ot

From Survival to Vocation

From Survival to Vocation

The Radical and Relevant Call of the
Gospel in Times of Chaos and Peril

WAYNE L. MENKING

Foreword by Kristin Johnston Largen

WIPF & STOCK · Eugene, Oregon

FROM SURVIVAL TO VOCATION
The Radical and Relevant Call of the Gospel in Times of Chaos and Peril

Copyright © 2023 Wayne L. Menking. All rights reserved. Except for brief quotations in critical publications or reviews, no part of this book may be reproduced in any manner without prior written permission from the publisher. Write: Permissions, Wipf and Stock Publishers, 199 W. 8th Ave., Suite 3, Eugene, OR 97401.

Wipf & Stock
An Imprint of Wipf and Stock Publishers
199 W. 8th Ave., Suite 3
Eugene, OR 97401

www.wipfandstock.com

PAPERBACK ISBN: 978-1-6667-3648-9
HARDCOVER ISBN: 978-1-6667-9482-3
EBOOK ISBN: 978-1-6667-9483-0

01/30/23

The Scripture quotations contained herein are from the New Revised Standard Version Bible, copyright © 1989 by the Division of Christian Education of the National Council of Churches of Christ in the U.S.A., and are used by permission. All rights reserved.

Dedicated to the people of Mora and San Miguel Counties in New Mexico, the victims of the Hermit's Peak/Calf Canyon Fires in the spring and summer of 2023, and the many individuals and organizations who are giving of themselves to help rebuild lives, livelihoods, homes, and communities after the fire's decimating devastations.

Contents

Foreword by Kristin Johnston Largen | ix
Preface | xi
Acknowledgements | xix
Abbreviations | xxiii

Part I: The World We Live In: Between Death and Life
  1 The Power of Death Is Closer Than We Thought | 3
  2 Life in Survival Mode: Driven by Unregulated Fear | 18
  3 The Empowering but Unsettling Hope of the Gospel | 40

Part II: Becoming What We Are Yet to Be
  4 What God, Lord, or Power Defines Your World? | 63
  5 Living into Vocation: Life under the Cross | 80
  6 Led into Liminality with Only Hope and Prayer: The Security of a Beggar | 107
  7 Nourished into New Imagination | 132

Bibliography | 147

Foreword

No one needs to be told that this is somewhat of a liminal time for the church; some might say this is a liminal time for the whole of the United States as well. Coming out of the pandemic (and into a COVID-endemic period of uncertain duration) and all of the disruptions and eruptions that occurred during these past two years, many are looking forward into an uncertain future with no small amount of trepidation.

It is not clear what shape the church is going to take in the next ten, twenty, thirty years. Many congregations are shrinking; all congregations are changing. How should we respond? How are we to feel? How are we to continue the walk of faithful discipleship to Jesus Christ?

In this paralyzing climate of anxiety and fear, Wayne Menking has written a book that seeks to offer a path forward characterized by trust in God, confidence in the power of the Holy Spirit, and reliance on core Lutheran theological doctrines that continue to offer practical insights for Christian life in the world today. Menking challenges the reader to move out of "survival mode," a mode characterized by a desperate need to control, a fight-or-flight mentality, and the tendency to dehumanize those with whom we disagree, those who feel threatening to us. He describes this mode as "idolatrous," as it turns us inward, away from God and the neighbor, and keeps the focus on ourselves and our own desires and beliefs. This is, in Menking's words, "narcissistic self-absorption," and it is never life-giving, it is only death-dealing.

Foreword

Instead, then, Menking invites the reader to lean confidently into the future: the book is forward-thinking and forward-looking; it extends an invitation to view the future with hope and the confident expectation that comes from a sure faith in the God who is continually doing a new thing.

Menking uses the work of Jürgen Moltmann, particularly Moltmann's description of the contrast between "a religion of death" and "a culture of life." This quote is characteristic of the argument Menking constructs: "What is needed . . . is a culture of life that is stronger than the terror of death, a love for life that overcomes the destructive forces in our world today, a confidence in the future that overcomes doubt and fatalism." (Chapter 1) This is Christian hope grounded in the reality of God's transformative mercy and grace; it is clear-eyed, neither denying nor downplaying current challenges, but also insistent that God is at work bringing good out of evil, leading us along a way where life and life abundant await—not just for me, but for us all, together.

Menking uses basic Lutheran insights, including a theology of the cross and Luther's explications in the Large Catechism, as a way to both explicate and inspire a faith that is courageous, bold, and outward-facing. In particular, he describes an expanded view of salvation that is not privatized but includes the other, such that we see and embrace Christ's saving love of the neighbor and the stranger as a part of our own salvation story. This understanding of salvation highlights the contrast between a life of discipleship to the gospel of Jesus Christ, and a life enslaved to the narcissistic suspicion and contempt that characterizes so much in contemporary culture.

The book concludes with a description of the sacraments as "sustaining nourishment that propel us into God's future and new creation." (Chapter 7) In this liminal moment, Christians are fed and nourished by Jesus Christ's own body and blood, strengthened for service through the power of the Holy Spirit, and called to step boldly into a future characterized by God's creativity and new life. This call is not without risk and challenge, but in the shadow of God's wings and inspired by the Spirit, we walk with confidence, trusting in the One who goes before us to prepare the way. This is the way of Christian hope; this is the way of life.

Kristin Johnston Largen
President, Wartburg Theological Seminary

Preface

WE LIVE IN VERY troubled, chaotic, and perilous times, where life as we have known it is threatened on different fronts. Devastating fires along with intensifying destructive weather patterns confront us with the realities of global warming and environmental devastations. Increased political divisions along with conspiracy theories and insurrections confront us with the extent to which the stability of our trusted forms of governance are vulnerable to authoritarianism and anarchy. Gun violence has taken away our innocent trust of being able to walk safely in our neighborhoods or go about our business. Racism and white supremacy have reared their heads with intensity, if in fact, they ever went away. And if all of that isn't enough, the pandemic and its indiscriminate attack on global health, global economies, and life itself have brought us face to face with the truth of just how fragile life is, and how near death really is. In the face of these daunting threats the spoken and unspoken anxiety is how do we survive and return to the normal life in which we have had security and well-being. This anxiety is true for individuals and institutions, including local congregations and the church.

For many in these unsettling times, the gospel is a message of palliative comfort. The word from many pulpits is that regardless of what may surround us, "be assured that you are loved and held by God." While there is an undeniable truth to this assertion, it is also an assurance that wittingly or unwittingly supports the palliative belief that God will eventually return

Preface

things to normal; all we have to do is wait patiently (and passively). What is missing is the gospel's central message, "Behold I make all things new!" In fact, the entire biblical story, from the Exodus to the gospel narrative of Jesus' death and resurrection is that God is always leading people from what is old into what is new! The title of this book is intended to convey that message! The circumstances in which we presently find ourselves are not the occasion for asking how to survive or how we return to the safety and security of what is settled and old; rather it is a time to awaken ourselves to the fact that we are in a moment where what has been safe, secure, familiar, and known is giving way to something that is new, even if we do not yet know what that new looks like. Moreover, what is old and giving way to what is new is doing so in ways that are disruptive, unnerving, and even painful. The importance and necessity of survival in these difficult times is neither denied or discounted in this discussion. Survival is critical and necessary, especially for those living at the margins of life. The notion of survival in this book will be a specific reference to the physical, emotional, and spiritual energy that is invested in preserving and holding on to what is familiar, comfortable, safe, what we have known and are familiar with from the past, and our efforts to return life to normal and the status quo. This specific form of survival energy is not life giving, but rather keeps us out of our vocation to care for neighbor. For persons who lay claim to a faith and trust in the gospel of Jesus the Christ, this is not a time to be asking "How we are to survive so that we can have life as it has been?" Rather it is a time to be asking the more life giving question, "What is our vocation and what does it mean to live into God's new creation and future in these perilous times?"

I approach this discussion and write out of my Lutheran theological tradition, a tradition grounded in Luther's distinction between a theology of the cross and a theology of glory and for which the priority of vocation over survival (as we are describing it) is of utmost importance. It will reference Luther throughout the discussion, especially his instruction in the Large Catechism. Please be assured that in no way is this intended to turn readers into Lutherans or to make a defense for Lutheran theology. It is intended, though, to offer persons who are grappling with the relevance of their Christian faith in these difficult times an honest and candid assessment of the travails and perils that are threatening us, and at the same time the honest and candid perspective that the Christian faith has always been a message of hope situated in a context of peril—a hope that always leads to vocation, not survival! Paradoxically, this faith has always held to the deep belief that Jesus' brutal death and life giving resurrection is the very Word that brings forth life in the midst of death. It is this conviction that defined and led early Christians and followers of Jesus, empowering them to follow the way of the cross into their vocational calling of proclaiming and living God's Kingdom of justice and mercy in the face of the threats and perils they faced. With this in mind, the intent of this book is to help the reader see that the Christian faith is still about following the way of the cross into vocation, especially in difficult and trying times. It is a vocation that is always expressed in the simple yet complex and often misunderstood words of Jesus, "You shall love your neighbor as yourself!" This is not charitable volunteerism. It is a vocation that calls us to stand in solidarity with our neighbors in the face of suffering and death.

So why approach this discussion through the lens of Luther's Large Catechism? A fair question. For starters, I'm a Lutheran and have been all my life. I grew up in a Lutheran pastor's family, was baptized and confirmed a Lutheran. Confirmation was an important milestone in my early adolescent years. I went to a Lutheran college and a Lutheran seminary. While these early years are foundational for me, my own faith has grown and matured in the ongoing discovery of what I perceive to be the meaning of the biblical narrative's central message, "Behold I make all things new." It is the message of the prophets as they warned Judah and Israel of their impending punishment. It is the core message of the gospel, powerfully spoken in the life, death and resurrection of Jesus, and declared again by Paul, "If anyone is in Christ, a new creation!" From my perspective, this is the gospel's most powerful message. In spite of ourselves and what we are doing to each other and the earth, we along with all of creation are daily being made new, even as we encounter suffering and death. It is also my perspective that Luther's chief aim in writing the Large Catechism was to articulate and communicate this core message, particularly in light of his observation of how extensively the faith was being abusively lived and practiced when he made parish visitations in the fall of 1528. So make no mistake; he did not write this instruction as a new or romanticized way to improve or enhance one's personal or privatized faith. Nor did he write it to offer a new way of becoming better moral or religious human beings. He wrote it to instruct baptized believers about what it means to *live and practice the life of faith as beings and participants in the kingdom of God and the new creation in the here and now and in the face of the enormous powers of evil and death! In this discussion, it is what we will refer to as the life and practice of being a culture of life in the face of the demonic and evil powers that threaten us.*

For Luther this new creation—this culture of life—is both now and not yet. It is God's future that has been inaugurated in the life, death, and resurrection of Jesus. It is a future that is here and now, incomplete though it may be; it is a future that is coming towards us, yet one that compels us to believe it in such a way that we practice living and being in it now, especially with the powers of death being as fierce as they seem to be.

To better understand the importance and relevance the instruction of Luther's Large Catechism offers our particular context, it is helpful to understand the immediate context and circumstances to which he was writing. Not long after the church in Saxony had been freed from Rome's oppressive rule and its reform and oversight had been given to the Elector, John of Saxony, parish visitations were conducted by Luther and some of his colleagues between October 1528 and January of 1529. The purpose of these visits was to evaluate the state of the church, or perhaps more accurately stated, to evaluate the state of faith and how it was being practiced and lived. What Luther encountered was dismal. Hear words from his Preface to the Small Catechism.

> The deplorable conditions which I recently encountered when I was a visitor constrained me to prepare this brief and simple catechism or statement on Christian teaching. Good God, what wretchedness I beheld! The common people, especially those who live in the country have no knowledge of Christian teaching, and unfortunately many pastors are quite incompetent and unfitted for teaching. Although the people are supposed to be Christian, are baptized, and receive the holy sacrament, they do not know the Lord's Prayer, the Creed, or the Ten Commandments, they live as if they were pigs and irrational beasts, and now that the gospel has been restored they have mastered the fine art of abusing liberty.[1]

On the surface, Luther's words may well sound judgmental and condemning. Yet, I suggest they are profoundly pastoral. Pastoral because they also reveal the deep grief and concern he felt over the poverty and ignorance of the faith and its practice in the lives of persons who laid claim to being baptized Christians. He realized that they had no clue to what that identity meant for the ordinary affairs of their life and their relationships with each other. I further suggest that it is precisely this core pastoral heart

---

1. Tappert, *Book of Concord,* 338.

Preface

and concern that compels us to return to his instruction so as to hear its wisdom—not as a set of rules, dos, and don'ts, but more as a handbook or manual that will assist us to live out our faith in the midst of the perils and threats confronting us. To be sure, Luther's instruction in his Large Catechism will often sound like a religious set of dos and don'ts. At times, the hierarchical, socio-culture norms of his time will sound offensive and abrasive to our ears. As you the reader will see throughout this discussion, the importance of Luther's instruction may not be what first appears on the surface; it will be in both the prophetic and pastoral concerns that lie below the surface. It is my hope that this discussion brings those concerns to the fore.

Yes, there is an implication that I am making, and I make it without apology. In our self- absorbed narcissistic culture, we are not that far removed from what Luther experienced in his parish visitations. Many in our culture lay claim to being baptized Christians and proudly bear its banner, yet have no clue whatsoever to what that identity means for their life and their relationships with their neighbor and the world, no clue to what the gospel is actually calling us to be and become. My profound hope is that this discussion will help open the eyes, hears, and hearts of all of us so as to see and understand through the eyes of Luther's instruction, the gospel's radical and relevant call on our lives, especially in these difficult times.

For many, using a catechism or catechetical instruction as a resource for helping us navigate the practice of our faith in perilous times will sound strange. And why not? After all, regardless of one's tradition or denomination, catechisms are usually viewed as teachings relegated to the instruction of children and young adults on the rudiments of the faith and to their preparation for the rite of confirmation. Once confirmed, it's as though the instruction is "one-and-done." As adults we don't pay much attention, if any at all, to catechisms. Or as Luther suggested, its as if we think we have outgrown them.[2] Hear his words about disregarding and ignoring the need for daily study, meditation, and reflection on this rudimentary instruction.

> Besides, a shameful and insidious plague of security and boredom has overtaken us. Many regard the Catechism as a simple, silly teaching which they can absorb and master in one reading. After reading it once they toss the book into a corner as if they are ashamed to read it again.[3]

2. Tappert, *Book of Concord*, 359.
3. Tappert, *Book of Concord*, 359

But then he cuts to the chase to reveal the real reason daily study, meditation, and reflection are so vital for the life of faith. Referring to those who think they have the catechism mastered, or for those who think they have no further need of the Catechism's wisdom once it has been read, he says:

> I implore them not to imagine that they have learned these parts of the Catechism perfectly, or at least sufficiently, even though they think they know them ever so well. Even if their knowledge of the Catechism were perfect (though that is impossible in life), yet it is highly profitable and fruitful daily to read it and make it the subject of meditation and conversation. In such conversation, reading, and meditation the Holy Spirit is present and bestows ever new and greater light and fervor, so that day by day we relish and appreciate the Catechism more greatly . . . Nothing is so effectual against the devil, the world, the flesh, and all evil thoughts so as to occupy oneself with the Word of God, talk about it, and meditate on it. Psalm 1 calls those blessed who "meditate on God's law day and night." You shall never offer up any incense or other savor more potent against the devil than to occupy yourself with God's commandments and words and to speak, sing, and meditate on them This, indeed, is the true holy water, the sign which routs the devil and put him to flight.[4]

And therein lies the heart and core of why daily meditation and reflection on the Catechism is so vital to us now. While not a substitute for Holy Scripture, Luther's catechetical instruction was and is both the essence and a pathway through which the Word of God is communicated and through which it addresses the human heart and spirit. More directly to the point, such daily meditation and reflection is the means through which baptized believers are equipped and empowered to resist the powers of evil and death. It is for this reason that I approach this discussion on the gospel's radical and relevant call in these times of peril, chaos, and threat through the lens of Luther's instruction in the Large Catechism. It is an instruction to equip and empower us to resist the powers of evil and death that are threatening us in these days. Indeed, just as it was for Luther and the church to which he was writing, the stakes are quite high.

As you, the reader, will see in this discussion, one of my key assertions is that we can no longer hear the gospel—or Luther's instruction—through the lens of our settled and familiar religious formulae. Rather it is a time to listen and absorb the questions our faith is asking of us, and to open

---

4. Tappert, *Book of Concord*, 359–60

Preface

ourselves to where those questions are leading us. Lest you wonder where this assertion comes from, let me assure you that writing this book was not easy; for in reading and studying the catechism yet again, I found my own faith and how I have practiced it consistently questioned and challenged. It forced me to look at how I have taken my faith in God, Jesus, and the Spirit for granted. I trust you may well have the same experience. But I also trust that if you allow yourself to sit with whatever questions emerge, or allow yourself to sit with the discomfort of being challenged or questioned, you may also find that you are being encountered by the Spirit, albeit perhaps not as you might have expected. I pray that in and through all of this, you will be led to new visions and imaginations of what it means for you to live into the new creature you are becoming, to live into your baptismal vocation of loving your neighbor as yourself in these difficult and trying times.

One brief and final comment. You, the reader, will notice that while references to Luther's Large Catechism abound throughout this text, there is no appendix in which a reference copy of it is included. I have used Kirsi Stjerna's, *The Large Catechism of Dr. Martin Luther 1529*, as my reference throughout this book. Bibliographical information is included in Abbreviations. Other editions of the Large Catechism—and the Small Catechism—are available, some of which can be found online. I leave it to you to obtain a copy as you see fit or feel the need. My prayer is that this discussion will then be a lens through which to understand and apply Luther's instruction to your living and practicing of the faith in these perilous times.

May the Spirit of truth, power, and grace guide you in your reading, your meditation, your reflection, and above all, in your pilgrimage of leaving survival for vocation.

Wayne Menking
The Season of Pentecost
Fall, 2022

Acknowledgements

THOUGHTS, IDEAS, AND INSPIRATIONS don't turn into books without a cadre of people who are willing to share with an author the arduous pilgrimage of turning those thoughts, ideas, and inspirations into words and speech. Sometimes what this cadre gives is affirmation and encouragement; sometimes it is the challenge of questions that have not been thought about or spoken; sometimes it is a confrontation with a truth that that has been hidden or denied. Sometimes it is their willingness to reveal part of themselves and the "stuff" they are living and wrestling with on a daily basis. And perhaps more importantly it is their willingness to let you expose yourself—what you are feeling and thinking, what you are living with, what risks and vulnerabilities you are feeling as you put thoughts into words for others to read and consider. Sometimes it is is their willingness and patience to let you be wrong, go down a misdirected path, or to sit with thoughts that are hanging and unfinished. I cannot say thank you enough to those who have shared in the pilgrimage of bringing this book to life.

I am grateful to Don Breland, long time ACPE colleague and retired Army chaplain. Don first shared the story of his experience with a captured North Vietnamese soldier during a time of reflection and meditation in a group we were in together (shared in the first chapter). I never forgot the story, nor its impact on me and those who were in the room. I am most grateful not only for the consultation and encouragement he offered in the

Acknowledgements

writing of this book, but for the risks he has taken and his faithfulness to his vocational call as a chaplain, a pastor, and an educator.

Likewise, I am deeply appreciative of Dr. Javier Alanís, a colleague and former professor and director at the Lutheran Seminary Program of the Southwest, now the Centro Teológico Luterano Multicultural. Javier is a life long Lutheran who has lived in borderland reality all of his life. He is a masterful scholar who has made important contributions to interpreting Lutheran theology in the context of that reality. His insights on the truths of borderland reality, reflected on his website noted in the bibliography, along with his consultation and encouragement, proved most helpful in my discussion of the realities in which we are situated as we live in a world of "otherness" and cultural diversity.

Dr. Craig Nessan of Wartburg Theological Seminary is a colleague with whom I have been able to share many conversations, all of which usually leave me with a thought or insight I hadn't had before, thoughts and insights that stick with me and inspire me to pursue them further. I am grateful for the affirmation, encouragement, and consultation he extended on this pilgrimage.

Dr. Kristin Johnston Largen is the President of Wartburg Theological Seminary. I am deeply appreciative for her willingness to take the time to write the foreword for this book. Such an undertaking requires time to read the work, digest it, give thought to what one wants to say about it, and then write. All of that she graciously consented to do in the midst of her very busy schedule, and for that I am most grateful.

Dr. Phil Ruge-Jones, former religion professor at Texas Lutheran University and now pastor at Grace Lutheran Church in Eau Claire, Wisconsin, offered guidance and consultation when this project was in its infancy. I am appreciative for his help in giving my initial thinking clarity, focus, and direction, and for his encouragement in motivating me to take the steps to move this project forward.

Two synodical bishops of the ELCA, Bishop Erik Gronberg and Bishop Michael Reinhardt, graciously offered their consultation and encouragement. Their pastoral and theological insights with regard to the struggles of the church in our present contexts were most helpful. I am equally grateful for their collegiality and for their candid engagements with me around this project and its focus.

To my ACPE colleagues and educators who along the way have been instrumental in guiding me into the vocation of listening to the sufferings

Acknowledgements

of others, I extend a heartfelt thanks. Through their wisdom and experience, they've taught me much about myself, about justice, equity and what it means to live in community. In particular, I am grateful to Alicia Po Ching and Kofi Adzaku. Both are significant colleagues who have shared in the pilgrimage of leaving survival for vocation, and for their collegiality in this journey, I am most grateful.

Perhaps the most significant contributors to the writing of this book are the participants in a study group on Luther's Large Catechism. This was a group that came together at my invitation to engage in study, reflection, and discussion on Luther's instruction; we met twice a month for over a year and a half. These are people of faith who come from a multitude of occupations and careers. Some are retired, others are almost retired, and others are active in their occupations. Their commonality, though, is in the faith they share and the commitments they have to living that faith in daily life and amid all that we are living with in these days. The group participants were Stan and Mary Weiss, Katrina Martich, Christina Miller, Chris Forte, Ruth and Mark Vinceguerra, Medric Rogers (now deceased), Patti and Chuck Brunnert, and Gilda Harvey. I can't thank these people enough for their time and investment in this project, not to mention their enduring patience with me, and their willingness to engage the difficult questions and issues with which we are now facing. To all of you I extend a heartfelt thanks, and I especially give thanks to God for your commitments to the faith and the vocational life in which all of you are engaged.

It cannot go without being said that even though family members may not make direct contributions to the research or writing of a book, books don't get written without their involvement. In some ways, families live with the project as much as the author. And for all their willingness to live with this project, and with me, during its writing, I am deeply indebted to my family! To my children who through their lives continue to teach me a great deal about living in the vocation of parenting, I can't thank you enough. But more importantly, I am grateful for being able to watch all of you grow and mature into your own vocational lives as you live in this difficult and complex world. I hope you know how grateful I am and how much I keep learning from you. And to my spouse, Nancy, whose endless patience and willingness to give space and time for this project made it all possible. As with my children, Nancy teaches me a great deal about living in the complexities and difficulties of life, differing though our perspectives might be at times. I am profoundly grateful and thankful that I share life with you.

Abbreviations

LW   Luther, Martin. *Luther's Works*. Edited by Jaroslav Pelikan, Helmut T. Lehmann. Philadelphia: Fortress and St. Louis: Concordia, 1955-.

TLC   Stjerna, Kirsi. *The Large Catechism of Dr. Martin Luther 1529*. The Annotated Luther Study Edition. Minneapolis: Fortress, 2016.

Part I

The World We Live In
Between Death and Life

1

The Power of Death Is Closer Than We Thought

A Culture of Life in the Face of Death

ALL OF LIFE, WHETHER animal, plant, or human being, is always situated in the precarious place between death and life. Living in this in-between place is inescapable. Hard as we might try to control life so as to protect ourselves from death's ever present power, we cannot. Ask anyone who has unexpectedly lost a child or a loved one in a natural disaster, through devastating illness, a traumatic accident, or violence. From the moment of our birth, we live in this vulnerable place. At times death's presence and the vulnerability we feel around it are more intense and real than at others. Much of the time, though, we are able to go through life without giving death's presence attention, putting it off as something that will happen in the distant future.

On the surface, this assertion will sound like an auspiciously depressing way to start a book. The central theme throughout this discussion is that we are living in very perilous and chaotic times, a threatening age where death's presence is real and close. If we are listening, it is an age that is awakening us to the urgency of the gospel's radical call to leave our controlling, survival modes of living to engage the hope filled vocational life into which all Christians have been baptized. It is the vocational life Jesus summed up when he was asked which law was the most important; his reply, "You shall

Part I: The World We Live In

love the Lord your God with all your heart, soul, and mind, and you shall love your neighbor as yourself." At the same time it will assert that stepping into this life and call is not as easy as it may sound. It is not a call to a new kind of charitable volunteerism. Rather it is a call into a vocation that asks us to leave our settled and familiar ways of living, having life and protecting ourselves, to venture into the unknown, uncertain, and disorientating place of suffering and dying. Why? Because to love one's neighbor as one's self cannot authentically happen until we acknowledge that the realities and threats of suffering and death encompass all of us, not just a few of us.

A brief story will illustrate. It is a story shared by a colleague and friend who is now a retired Army chaplain as well as a retired Certified Educator of ACPE, Inc. The story took place while he was serving as a chaplain in Vietnam.[1] He tells of being with his battalion as it was involved in a brutal battle with North Vietnamese soldiers, a battle with intense gun fire and shelling that lasted about twenty four hours with each side suffering significant casualties and loss of life. For both sides of the battle, death was close at hand. If one has never been in such a place, it is difficult to imagine the sounds and acrid smells of constant mortar fire and the images of bodies being ripped apart. Even more, it is difficult to imagine the deep horror, terror, and fear that fills the human spirit, for each human being on both sides of the battle. But those deep feelings engender something else as they always do in a fight or a war. In the intensity of battle, being shot at, and facing death, feelings of hate towards the enemy emerge and intensify, feelings that evolve into a contemptuous disregard for their life and an intense desire to destroy them. It is a feeling on both sides. When this feeling and spirit of dehumanization takes over, the desire to kill can consume one's body, soul, and heart. It's what happens when death becomes close and real. When death comes this close and unleashes its power, it is as though God is nowhere to be found. In this place of dehumanizing killing, the human mind cannot imagine or conceive it as a place where God could even exist! It is the opposite. It is pure hell!

Eventually, the battalion surrounded the North Vietnamese and they surrendered. Those who surrendered were taken as prisoners and placed in a cordoned off holding area. As my chaplain friend walked around the area's perimeter, checking to see if the prisoners were being properly treated, checking to see whether any had particular needs, one of the North

---

1. Don Breland, (Chaplain, US Army, Retired), story shared in phone discussion with author, October 2021.

The Power of Death Is Closer Than We Thought

Vietnamese prisoners noticed the cross on his helmet. Through an interpreter, the prisoner asked if the chaplain would come over to talk with him. My friend responded, walking as close as he could get to him without crossing the cordoned-off area. As he knelt down, the soldier asked him, "Does the cross on your helmet mean you are a Christian?" After hearing that it did, the soldier said, "I am a Christian, too." It seems almost impossible that two people who only hours before had been on the opposite sides of such an intense and dehumanizing battle would find commonality, much less a commonality in their Christian faith.

Realizing they were of the same faith, the soldier shared his fears and concerns of what might happen to him. We can imagine that after all he had been through and now being held captive, he was living with a deep fear for what might happen to his life, whether or not he might in fact be tortured or killed. Hearing and understanding the man's fear of what might be ahead of him, the chaplain tried to assure him as best as he could that he would be treated humanely. After a while, the chaplain asked him "Your faith is important to you; what meaning does it have for you right now?" The soldier responded, "When I left to go to war, my grandmother told me that Jesus would keep me safe." I can imagine that in this moment, the soldier might have been wondering if his grandmother had told him the truth. Recalling this encounter, my chaplain friend said, "It was a profound and emotional moment for both of us." They talked a while more, and then he prayed with the soldier. He was eventually taken away, and my friend never saw him again.

Three things stand out in this powerful story. The first is that every human being situated in this battle stood in the dread-filled space between life and death, with the balance significantly tipping towards death rather than life. The second is that in this frightening place of death and hell, God was present—and recognized! God was recognized, not in images of glorious and majestic splendor or triumph but in the image of a cross, which interestingly enough is in and of itself an image of death—a brutal and dehumanizing death at that! The third is that in the midst of this battlefield's dehumanizing environment, and in the midst of this soldier's intense fear over what might happen to him, my chaplain friend humanized him. That is, he recognized him as a fellow human being, somebody just like himself who is situated between death and life, not immune from death's power and threats. With that recognition he honored the soldier with a listening ear and a compassionate heart. He did not make judgment on him nor did he discredit or discount his experience; he simply listened and as best as he could, he stood in solidarity with his suffering. It cannot go unrecognized that the humanization and solidarity my friend offered this soldier required him to take the risk of stepping out of his comfort zone into an unknown place with a total stranger who only hours before had been the enemy. The vocation of loving one's neighbor as one's self cannot be more vividly exemplified.

The German theologian, Jürgen Moltmann puts this into perspective. He observes that in our present moment, we are living in what he calls a "religion of death." Not unlike the battlefield, it is a perilous environment where "life is no longer loved, accepted, or affirmed."[2] We might say that it is no longer humanized. What is needed, Moltmann says is "a culture of life that is stronger than the terror of death, a love for life that overcomes the destructive forces in our world today, a confidence in the future that overcomes doubt and fatalism."[3] I suggest that that culture of life is exactly what my chaplain friend represented and gave when he compassionately humanized the imprisoned soldier. In his solidarity with the soldier's suffering, he affirmed his life and faith, he gave him a hope to face his fears and terrors. In the face of all the perils we face, Christians are being called by the gospel to be a culture of life that is stronger than the terror of death and to have a love for life that will overcome the destructive power of death that presently confronts and threatens us. We are being called to offer a love for life that will humanize those who are dehumanized, to offer an acceptance and affirmation of those who have been relegated and disenfranchised to the margins of life.

The Religion of Death

The power of the religion of death cannot be over estimated or over stated. One of its universal manifestations is in the form of terrorism and suicidal killings. Terrorism is a kind of ideology that values death more than life. It sees taking the life of another as having a God-like power over life and death. This is a reality that is not distantly isolated "over there" in a country besieged by perpetual civil war and disorder, nor is it a reality perpetuated by a specific religion. It exists here in our own backyards, in our cities, neighborhoods, schools, shopping malls, and theaters. Parents can

2. Moltmann, *Spirit of Hope*, 4.
3. Moltmann, *Spirit of Hope*, 3.

no longer send their children to school without the anxiety of a random shooter showing up to do his damage. One cannot go to any public gathering without concern or anxiety about what crazed person with a weapon will show up to take as many lives as he can. Moltmann accurately observes:

> It is not possible to deter suicidal assassins, for they have broken the fear of death. They do not love life anymore, and they want to die with their victims... This apocalyptic "religion of death" is the real enemy of the will to live, the love of life, and the affirmation of being.[4]

Suicidal assassins and random shooters are not the only manifestations of a religion of death. As Moltmann rightly observes and as we have yet again been reminded by the eruption of war in Ukraine, the threat of nuclear war and its devastations are alive and real. Not unlike terrorists and suicidal assassins, the threat of nuclear warfare is not just in the weapons themselves; it is in the people whose hands and fingers are on the triggers and buttons that initiate their use. When leaders making the decisions about whether or not to pull the trigger have no regard for life or whose fear of death has been broken, they take on a God-like power that brings death closer than we thought or want.

The religion of death has another manifestation that on the surface appears less violent and hostile, yet in its own way brings death to many, if not physically, then surely through the dehumanization and exploitation it inflicts. It is what Moltmann refers to as "social misery," which he observes, is brought on by the ever widening gap between the rich and the poor, the haves and the have-nots.[5] Like terrorism, it is not a misery that exists "over there" or in some distant place. It is in our own backyard, on our street corners, in homeless tent cities or any place a homeless person can find to sit, rest, or sleep. It is seen in border immigrant camps where persons with nothing wait, hoping to find their way into a place that will give them life, yet find themselves beleaguered by rules and laws that separate them from their children, or subjected to the brutalities of border street gangs taking advantage of their plight. It is wherever poverty and all of its devastations exist.

Moltmann's point is well taken. The threats of social misery are bad enough for the people who suffer in it. Its other threat, however, is that the widening gap between rich and poor, and the increasing disregard the rich

---

4. Moltmann, *Spirit of Hope*, 5.
5. Moltmann, *Spirit of Hope*, 6.

Part I: The World We Live In

have for the poor, threatens the very foundations of democracy. Democracies are premised on the idea that all share and strive for a common good, and all share in its fruits and benefits. When this balance is lost so that those on the bottom rungs of the ladder are falling off without notice or care from those on top, trust is lost and death comes closer to democracy than it thought.

Paradoxical as it may sound, the religion of death and its power are also manifested in those who are at the top rungs of the economic ladder, or those who are in pursuit of those top rungs. While their vulnerability may not be the same as those on the bottom, it is a vulnerability none the less. Those who persist in climbing the ladder to find and claim the life they think will give them ultimate satisfaction eventually discover that they are ensnarled in a relentless web of anxiety, a web from which they cannot escape and a web that often leads to death, whether physically, emotionally, or spiritually. It is an anxiety that eventually becomes "the anxiety of existence for modern human beings."[6]

The religion of death is manifested in another form of social misery, a misery deeply felt at every level of existence by those who have experienced and been the victims of dehumanization in any of its varied forms—racism and white supremacy, tribalism, hate and intolerance. Even if one is located in the middle rungs of the economic ladder or somewhere close to the top, yet is a person of color, a different sexual orientation, a different religion, or a person with mental illness, they know the experience of being dehumanized, looked upon with disdain and having their integrity and dignity as a human being looked upon with suspicion, doubt or complete disregard! To know the experience of being dehumanized is to know death, and sometimes that death is physical and brutal as in the inproportionate numbers of African American men killed either by white policemen or white vigilantes testifies, men such as Ahmaud Arbery and George Floyd. To know dehumanization is to live with the fear that as a person of color living in a white neighborhood you can't walk down your own street without being suspected of a criminal activity. To know dehumanization is to know the searing pain felt by a Haitian immigrant being horsewhipped by a border patrol agent on horseback. To know dehumanization is to be an American citizen of Mexican descent serving in the U.S. military, yet while in uniform be accused of being an undocumented and illegal immigrant. To know dehumanization is to know that your transgendered child is being denied

---

6. Moltmann, *Spirit of Hope*, 7.

medical treatment and stigmatized for her condition. Dehumanization in whatever form it comes is not a one time incident. It is a constant power and threat whereby the individual or group being dehumanized is made to feel that they are of no regard, that their dignity and integrity as human beings is of no value or worth. It is a constant and prevailing threat to life!

The religion and power of death takes another form, our denial that global warming and the destruction of the environment are real, and our resistance to take steps to do anything about it. The effects of its devastations are not left to our imagination nor are they something that exist as a distant threat. We can see them in the hazed air that surrounds us, smell them in wild fire smoke that spreads thousands of miles from its origins. We can see see them in birds and fish killed by oil and washed up on our shores. We can see them in the extinction of species, water and crop shortages. Indeed the earth itself along with all of creation is groaning, a groaning to which we will not attune our ears. Just as the social miseries of the world have been brought on by the widening gaps and disparities between the rich and the poor, or more appropriately stated, by the disregard of those on top for those on the bottom rungs, the destruction of the earth and the resources it gives for life have been caused by humanity's disregard for the fact that the earth is literally our mother and our neighbor, that we are dependent on her for life. We have deluded ourselves into believing that the earth exists for us to do with what we want, that we are free to exploit it to serve our own purposes, arrogantly ignoring that our lives as human beings cannot exist without its sustenance. Without the earth and the biosphere that surrounds it, the human race dies! But just as devastating as the destruction of our earth home is the fact that humanity seems paralyzed or unwilling to do anything about it! Moltmann comments, "With some irony one may say: Some do not know what they are doing, while others do not act on what they know."[7] One might also say that our exploitation and abuse of our mother and neighbor earth is actually another form of dehumanization!

Numbed to Death's Presence and Power

Everything noted above will surely sound like an unsettling litany of death, especially to ears that are accustomed to the sounds of positive and upbeat preaching that focuses on personal salvation yet tends to minimize the gravity and power of death's threatening existence. Others will likely hear

7. Moltmann, *Spirit of Hope*, 8.

Part I: The World We Live In

it as a dour and hopeless projection of the future of life and humanity to which we are resigned. Those reactions are understandable. The intent of what I've put forth, though, is to show the extent to which the powers of death are so very real close at hand, and more to show the extent to which we numb ourselves to their presence and threats.

Albeit our circumstances are quite different from post war Germany in 1945, we seem to have a similar posture towards death as that of the war's survivors. As a conscripted soldier who survived the war in an English prisoner of war camp, Moltmann recalls that "the survivors experienced the end of terror in 1945, but we had become so used to death that life took on a 'take it or leave it' atmosphere because it had become so meaningless."[8] Might it not be true that something similar is true for us. We are so used to seeing news reports that show us the tragedy and immense suffering of those whose lives have been devastated and destroyed that we have taken on what Moltmann observed in Germany, a "take it or leave it attitude." We have become narcotized and numb to the imminent presence of death's power and what it is doing to our neighbors, our sibling human beings, and to ourselves. This is particularly true in a culture of affluence and entitlement where every commodity, material possession, libation, and pleasure is readily available to help us avoid feelings of pain that come in our own sufferings, not to mention the pain we feel when we share in the sufferings and burdens of others. One can easily argue that more often than not, even Christian preaching avoids saying too much about suffering, opting instead to espouse positive and upbeat words that will inspire comfort and good feelings. Douglas John Hall, the noted Luther scholar now retired from McGill University in Toronto, rightly observes that Christians

> seem not to want to hear that anything is seriously wrong. Large numbers of people on this continent go to church for this precise reason of avoiding any such suggestion. They are quite literally seeking "sanctuary," a little island of calm way from the news broadcasts and urban squalor and graffiti where they can confirm their desperate determination to believe that "God's in his heaven, all's right with the world.[9]

But this is the point of our entire discussion. Numbing and narcotizing ourselves to the powers and threats of death that surround us are in reality a form of survival that take us out of the vocation of loving our neighbors

---

8. Moltmann, *Spirit of Hope*, 4.
9. Hall, *Imaging God*, 1.

as ourselves, the vocation to which the gospel of Jesus the Christ calls us. When we delude ourselves into believing that everything is okay with the world, even when it's not, we are not able to hear our neighbor's cry. Returning to the story of the chaplain and the captured soldier, we might well imagine that had the chaplain been numbed to the soldier's pains and fears, "believing that nothing was seriously wrong," he might have offered him a polite and charitable visit, but he would not have been able to stand with the man in his pain and angst. If he had numbed himself to the captured and imprisoned soldier's pain, he would never have been able to offer him a compassionate and humanizing presence.

Regardless of how being numbed comes about, whether in comfortable preaching that doesn't want to talk about suffering, whether in the consumer and materialistic drugs of our affluent culture, or simply in our desire to stay in safe, settled, and comfortable ways of life, we seem prone to seek a sanctuary that will protect and isolate us from the sufferings and pains of our neighbors and the world. I share two illustrations. A lay colleague was the pastoral associate of a congregation situated in a large populated urban area. While the congregation is somewhat mixed demographically, the primary movers and shakers are high functioning professionals in the corporate world where excellence is a high value. In their world, excellence is determined by outward appearances, by profit margins and return on investments for shareholders. In their church work, excellence is different, yet it carries the same expectations as their corporate world, namely present a brand and identity in the community that will make it attractive, appealing, and exude the appearance of success. From its state of the art music program, to its liturgical practices, to the quality of preaching that comes from its pulpit, excellence must be evidenced. However, as my colleague became acquainted with the real lived experiences of many of its members, she became increasingly aware that this pursuit of excellence, this attempt to create and present a brand, was in fact incongruent with the realities and lived experiences of many of its members. The physical persona of a successful and excellent church literally hid the shadow side of its membership, persons who were struggling and trying to find meaning and purpose in their life. Not only did it have difficulty connecting to the struggles of its own members, its connection to the suffering and pained community outside of its membership circles was diminished. The focus on the maintenance and preservation of its brand—survival!—detached the congregation from its vocational mission.

Part I: The World We Live In

The second illustration is not about a congregation. It is about a resistance existing in many white congregations to conversations relating to racism and white supremacy and their presence in the communal life of our congregations. Not long after the killing of Ahmaud Arbery, a group of pastors and lay persons in my denomination drafted a rather poignant and direct statement calling for congregations to engage in substantive conversations and to the work of dismantling racism and white supremacy. As one might expect, there was considerable reaction to the statement. One can understand the discomfort and anxiety that comes when we are urged to name and acknowledge that such things exist in our personal lives much less in our congregations and church life. Yet, the purpose of the statement was not to inflict shame. Rather it was to say that if we are to align ourselves with the victims of racial injustice and dismantle racism, white supremacy and all of their dehumanization, the first step is to name the disease within ourselves and our institutions. The same resistance can be seen when it comes to conversations on global warming, gun violence, and so many of the other issues that are threatening us. Not surprisingly and consistent with Hall's observation, we seem not to want to hear that anything is seriously wrong, and even more detrimental, we don't want to hear that we might be contributing to those wrongs.

The point to which all of this is leading is simply this. Moltmann's assertion that we live and are surrounded by a powerful religion of death that leads to resignation, powerlessness, and hopelessness is real! But just as real is his assertion that what is needed is a culture of life that is stronger than the terror of death, a love for life that overcomes the destructive forces in our world, and a confidence in a future that overcomes doubt and fear. If, as we said, the story of the chaplain with the imprisoned soldier is a paradigm for what this culture of life looks like, then the story reminds us that it is not about escaping, standing at a distance, or seeking some kind of transcendence from the powers of death. It is about standing together in solidarity with each other and our neighbor in the dread-filled spaces between death and life where death appears to have overpowered life. It is to stand in solidarity with our neighbor, wherever in the world that neighbor may be, believing that God is precisely in the place where we wonder if God has not abandoned us. In this regard, we follow Jesus to the cross.

A Way Into A Culture of Life—
Luther's Theology of the Cross

In the face of death's overwhelming powers, conventional religious wisdom and thinking looks for God to intervene with power and majestic glory to overcome and remove them. Or it simply offers a message that says God will keep us immune or offer a way for us to transcend those powers. This is especially so in our culture of affluence where triumph and success over adversity is of the highest value, and for many, a sign of God's favor. Conversely, our culture tends to view the inability to overcome suffering and adversity as a weakness, and for many, as a sign that the person in such a state doesn't have enough faith. But that's how conventional religious reasoning works. Simply put, it reasons that when things are prosperous and going well God is present and God is good; in times where adversity and suffering have been overcome, it reasons that God has heard our prayer, often with the sidebar thought that God rewarded our strong faith. And conversely, if our lives are not prosperous or we are unable to overcome adversity, we are left to believe that our faith has not been strong enough and we are not in God's favor. Luther called these ways of perceiving and reasoning God a theology of glory.[10] They are ways of reasoning that assume human beings can know the heart and mind of God. They are ways of reasoning that try to make sense or give meaning to real lived experiences that in truth make no sense or have no meaning at all. But this is what conventional religious wisdom and reasoning does: it tries to turn what is incomprehensible into something comprehensible so that it fits into our brain. When conventional religious wisdom can't make the incomprehensible comprehensible or when the incomprehensible is disruptive to our settled ways of life, it takes our mind off of it by calling it something else. It

---

10. Luther never published a treatise or document that specifically spelled out the difference between a *theology of the cross* and a *theology of glory*. However, it is a distinction that was interwoven throughout the fabric of his entire theological—and pastoral—perspectives on faith and life and how God is known. It is in the Heidelberg Disputation that he asserts this distinction, particularly in Theses 19, 20, 21, and 22: "(19) That person does not deserve to be called a theologian who looks upon the invisible things of God as though they were clearly perceptible in those things that have happened; (20) he deserves to be called a theologian, however, who comprehends the visible and manifest things of God seen through suffering and the cross; (21) a theologian of glory calls evil good and good evil. A theologian of the cross calls the thing what it is; (22) that wisdom that sees the invisible things of God in works as perceived by man is completely puffed up, blinded, and hardened" (LW 31:52–53).

gives us a message to avoid thinking about it, doesn't talk about it all, or it shames us into believing we have been hopelessly abandoned and must find a way to work ourselves out of the mess. Another way to think about this theology of glory is to call it a theology of control. That's what conventional religious wisdom and reasoning tell us: we can control whatever comes our way. And control is always driven by fear, a fear of the unknown, a fear of not knowing, or the fear that something will be lost.

For Luther, the opposite of this theology of glory is what he called a theology of the cross. Opposite a theology of glory and control, a theology of the cross is a theology of trusting when we have no control, especially no control over the powers of death. The truth and reality of human experience is what we have already described; it is the experience of knowing that suffering and death are closer than we thought or want to believe. It is knowing deep within our bones that we cannot control or overcome what those powers throw at us. It is the experience of being overwhelmed with powers and threats that are significantly larger and more powerful than we are, where our human strengths seem too small and limited to withstand what we are up against. In the face of these powers and our human limitations, pronouncements of "how great God is" or "how good God has been to me" are difficult if not impossible. In fact, it is in those moments that our human cry may well be the same as Jesus when he was feeling abandoned by God and dying on the cross, "My God, my God, why have you forsaken us?" A theology of the cross, as Luther asserts, sees, feels, and experiences something, then calls it what it is.[11]

The difficult truth is that God is not easy to find when we are in the throes of the powers of suffering and death, if at all. Like Jesus, the feeling that one has been abandoned to the powers of death is very real even if we try to conceal it. As hard as we might try to contain or deny our feelings and the cries that go with them, we cannot. For Luther, however, this place of feeling utterly abandoned and helpless, where God appears totally absent and AWOL, is precisely the place where God is, hidden and unavailable though she might appear. The difficulty is not that God has gone AWOL. The difficulty is that in these moments of abandonment, the eyes, ears, and reasonings of our theologies of glory are unable to comprehend God's heart, goodness, and love for humankind. For Luther, the heart, goodness and love of God can only be known through suffering and the cross. This

---

11. *LW* 31:53.

is why he called it a theology of the cross. Mary Solberg, now Professor Emeritus at Luther College, says it this way:

> The suffering of Christ upon the cross and his apparent abandonment by God, express God's judgment on human understandings of strength, wisdom, and justice. How could this be God's righteousness, this pathetic human being caught up in the weakness, the folly, and the injustice of an appalling crucifixion spectacle? This was more than a dichotomy between human and divine judgment; according to Luther this was God's way of frustrating the pretenses of human reason and judgment . . . The cross confounds the powers of human reason to make sense of it.[12]

The theology of the cross is good news in every sense of the word, even if its good news is hidden in what our senses and ways of reasoning appear as bad news. It is not the triumphalistic good news that the conventional religion and wisdom of our culture want to project and proclaim. The paradoxical good news of the gospel is that God has intervened into our world of death in the crucible form of death, a way totally foreign to our world's expectations of how a life-giving God is to be revealed. Think about it. God chooses to have her son born in poverty. He grows up to undertake God's mission by choosing disciples who are from the lowest echelons of society; his preaching is acclaimed by the poor, but he is so despised by the political and religious establishment that it not only discredits him, it seeks his death. Eventually the establishment wins; he dies a brutal, dehumanizing, and excruciating death on a cross, the most humiliating form of death known in the Roman world! This is not the life giving God we expect nor a God that our senses and ways of reasoning can readily see and validate. This is the strange and almost incomprehensible paradox of the Christian faith. In contrast to a theology of glory, this theology of the cross is an incomprehensible way of knowing and seeing God hidden in the places that appear to human reason as the least and most un-god like places for God to dwell, places like defeat, death, grief, wretchedness, and abandonment. The profound paradox of the cross is that the suffering and death of Jesus reveals God's life giving solidarity with humankind in its deepest miseries and sufferings, not in its highest, majestic, and glorious triumphs.

The cross turns everything upside down. The places that appear unrecognizable and totally unlike anything having to do with God are actually the places where God is. The places that appear to the intellect and

---

12. Solberg, *Compelling Knowledge*, 71.

Part I: The World We Live In

the prevailing powers and reasonings of the world as meek, worthless, and powerless are actually the places where God's creating and saving power is at work. What the world sees as foolishness and folly is actually wisdom; what the world sees as weakness and dishonorable is actually strong and honorable. James Cone, the now-deceased African American theologian and scholar, identifies this "foolishness" in the black experience of slavery and its identity with the cross of Jesus when he writes:

> That God could "make a way out of no way" in Jesus' cross was truly absurd to the intellect, yet profoundly real in the souls of black folk. Enslaved blacks who first heard the Gospel message seized on the power of the cross. Christ crucified manifested God's loving and liberating presence in the contradictions of black life—that transcendent presence in the lives of black Christians that empowered them to believe that ultimately, in God's eschatological future, they would not be defeated by the "troubles of this world," no matter how great and painful their suffering. Believing this paradox, this absurd claim of faith, was only possible through God's "amazing grace" and the gift of faith, grounded in humility and repentance. There was no place for the proud and the mighty, for people who think that God called them to rule over others. The cross was God's critique of power—white power—with powerless love, snatching victory out of defeat.[13]

Cone's words and the testimony of Black slaves and those who lived through the horrors of Jim Crow lynchings provide us with another real life meaning of the theology of the cross in our present perils. Parallel to the chaplain's story, they are a testimony to the power of the cross to give life in the face of death, to restore humanity in the face of dehumanization, a testimony that we desperately need in our present moment as we orient ourselves to what faith means and is calling us to in the realities of our present sufferings.

The truth is our present circumstances are nothing new in the life of the church. From its beginning the followers of Jesus have always known the threats of the daunting and overwhelming powers of death! And yet, they have held on to a faith and trust in the God who has strangely and paradoxically revealed herself in the very powers that stand opposite her, the powers of evil and death! Throughout its history and especially in its darkest moments, the church has been upheld and sustained by this belief. It is what has empowered her to remain faithful in her vocation, namely

13. Cone, *Cross and the Lynching Tree*, 2.

to be a culture of life, a community that stands solidarity with all who are overwhelmed by the powers of death. This does not mean that it has had unanimous and full agreement on every matter. The New Testament has plenty of examples of disagreements.[14] However, its unity was based on a spirit of love, which was not necessarily on having warm emotional feelings for each other, but rather a deep respect for each other's integrity, dignity, and human worth. And that respect was based solely on God's solidarity with humankind in the person, life, death, and resurrection of Jesus. It was this unity of spirit that held the church together as they faced, encountered, and engaged the powers of death that threatened them.

And so it is now. The powers of death are real and they are close at hand. However, if Luther's theology of the cross means anything in our present moment, it is this: if the powers of death are close at hand, then most assuredly so is God, for where death is, there God is, hidden, mysteriously creating and bringing life out of death even if we cannot see it, feel it, or know what it will look like. And if God is here and in solidarity with us, giving us life in the face of death, then, like the chaplain, we are called to be a culture of life that stands in solidarity with each other in the face of all the perils that threaten us. Being and living this culture of life and its solidarity with all of humankind in the face of death's power is the vocation to which the gospel radically calls us.

I close this chapter with Moltmann's powerful words:

> In the eternal yes of the living God, we affirm our fragile and vulnerable humanity in spite of death; in the eternal love of God, we love life and resist its devastations; in the ungraspable nearness of God, we trust in what is saving, even if the dangers are growing.[15]

---

14. Gal 2:11–14, NRSV.
15. Moltmann, *Spirit of Hope*, 14.

2

Life in Survival Mode
Driven by Unregulated Fear

Survival Mode—What Are We Talking About?

SURVIVAL IS A NATURAL human instinct that propels us to seek and protect life when we are under threat. It is propelled by fear, an emotion that is a natural part of our neurological make up; it is what warns us of the presence of a life threatening danger that warrants our taking steps to avoid it, or against which to defend ourselves. Countless are the stories where fear has empowered human beings or groups of people to survive insurmountable odds to live through the overwhelming powers of death. Countless, also, are the stories where groups of human beings have stepped through the threshold of fear to take risks to aid other human beings when their lives have been at risk or completely disrupted by natural disasters. One cannot and should not discredit the goodness and power that comes when human beings face the fear of death with courage and hope, or when groups of human beings rise to the occasion to help other human beings whose lives are at stake.

When natural disasters, accidents, or other unexpected disruptions shatter and destroy lives, their victims have little or no choice about what they hold on to or protect. If ordered to evacuate, they must leave behind much of what has defined their life with no certainty it will be there when the disaster has passed. In some cases, they are unable to protect and save loved ones. The power of the devastation will have its way, and they have no control over what it will do. Once the disaster or accident has passed, they are more often than not left to rebuild their life, which means living and moving into a new future that in the immediate present is uncertain. It is often a future that will not be like the past in that it may mean new surroundings, new housing, new jobs, new relationships, or even a life without valued possessions. Sometimes it is a future that will not include loved ones who died or were killed in the event. Regardless, what has been thrust on to these victims is the necessity of change, and change will inherently trigger feelings of fear. The past can be remembered and treasured, but it cannot be held on to or revived to what it was. The future into which they must now live will be new. What is required of them is to live into this unknown future with courage, resilience, and hope, fear filled though it may be. This is survival in the best sense of the word!

The survival mode of which we will speak in this chapter is very different: it is a mode of living precipitated and driven by unregulated fear, a fear that is self-preserving and self-protective. It anxiously—and sometimes desperately—seeks to control and hold on to an object or way of life out of fear that if that object or way of life is taken away, life will be diminished or at worst, there will be no life at all. It is a fear that triggers a fight-or-flight response, a response that more often than not leads to the dehumanizing of those we perceive to be a threat to our way of life or whatever we are desperately holding on to. A recent blog on the website, *Mastermind Connect,* by the attorney and wellness coach, LeMar Moore, aptly describes the survival mode we are talking about.

> Survival mode is the short term, fear based mode of thinking you enter when your fight-or-flight response is triggered. It's the poisonous mentality that leads you to attack or retreat during stressful times rather than communicate and embrace. In survival mode, you spend so much time focusing on the dangers that you miss out on the opportunities; you spend so much time cursing the bad things that happen to you that you miss the important lessons . . . Survival mode shuts off the part of you that takes risks, uses your imagination, and goes with the flow, and instead directs all that precious energy to the part that plays it safe, holds on to regret and resentment, and too often demands control. It's fine to go into this state if you're standing in front of a hungry mountain lion, but living in survival mode on a daily basis will exact a terrible toll on your mind, body and spirit over time.[1]

1. Moore, "Survival Mode," lines 1–12.

Part I: The World We Live In

Moore's description of fear-based survival existence is spot on. At the same time, it begs for a deeper understanding of how a natural and even God-given emotion can turn into something that is destructive and non life giving. In this regard, one such view that can be helpful is that of family systems theory, which understands that chronic anxiety is a deep and pervasive systemic force that weakens and deteriorates a society's capacity to regulate its instincts and emotions—like fear. When that capacity is diminished, it does not take long for the basic components that hold a society together to diminish: cooperation, cohesiveness, and altruism.[2]

Systems theory makes clear that chronic anxiety is not the same as the anxiety we think of when we say we are "feeling anxious," or when we might be having an "anxious day." Edwin Friedman describes chronic anxiety this way:

> It is a regressive emotional process that is quite different from the more familiar, acute anxiety we experience over specific concerns. Its expression is not dependent on time or events, even though specific happenings could seem to trigger it, and it has a way of reinforcing its own momentum. Chronic anxiety might be compared to the volatile atmosphere of a room filled with gas fumes, where any sparking incident could set off a conflagration, and where people would then blame the person who struck the match rather than trying to disperse the flames.[3]

Chronic anxiety is not limited to individual family units. Friedman went on to observe that the entire anxiety curve of entire civilizations go through periods when they rise or fall. He further observed that societies and civilizations lose their ability to cope with change when certain factors occur simultaneously:

> Anxiety escalates as society is overwhelmed by the quantity and speed of change; and the institutions or individuals (whether scapegoat or symptomatic) traditionally used to absorb or bind off society's anxiety are no longer available to absorb it.[4]

Seen through the lens of systems thinking, the behaviors to which Moore refers are the direct result of our society's diminished capacity to regulate its natural and God-given emotion of fear. And that diminished

---

2. Friedman, *Failure of Nerve*, 62.
3. Friedman, *Failure of Nerve*, 62.
4. Friedman, *Failure of Nerve*, 57.

capacity is the result of the onslaught with which change has come upon us with a rapidity that we cannot manage. Moreover, the institutions or individuals who absorbed that anxiety or helped us keep it at bay are no longer available, institutions like government or even religion. The upshot is that with the nearness of death being what it is, our fear has escalated and our ability to regulate that fear has diminished. It should not come as a surprise, then, that we have resorted to survival modes of living that in fact, do not preserve life at all, but contribute to its demise.

A Culture Stuck in Survival Mode

Ours is a culture situated in a fear-filled atmosphere. At the same time it is deceptive. On the one hand, life in this culture can be like floating down a peaceful looking river with a strong hidden undercurrent. On the surface it can feel beautiful, and inviting. On the other hand, below the surface there is an unseen but powerful and dangerous undertow. If you are unaware of its danger and not exercising caution, it can drag you into its powerful force without any warning. Once in its grasp, it's difficult to get free. This powerful undercurrent is fear, and its destructive effects are the very things Moore says are the patterns of a survival mode of existence. The escalating fear in our culture is creating a poisonous mentality that attacks or retreats rather than communicates or embraces; it is causing us to focus on perceived dangers and blaming each other for those dangers rather than search for opportunities that we can mutually embrace to alleviate those dangers. It is a fear that causes us to curse each other, especially those who we think are doing bad things to us, or those who don't see things our way. It is a fear that is paralyzing our imaginations, causing us to play it safe rather than take risks; it is a fear that causes us to hold on to regret and anger rather than forgive and step into new futures. Above all, it is a fear that makes us try and control what we cannot control, a fear that causes us to try and control or manipulate others into our ways of thinking.

As the chaos and perils around us have exponentially increased, and as the intensity of the conversations around those perils has likewise increased, that fear has escalated and taken many forms. It is a fear dividing us in all quarters of our life together, including our life together in faith communities and Christian congregations.

When COVID-19 invaded our life the fear in our culture became palpable. The fear of contacting the disease and the fear of not having a known way to stop it or treat it was a deep angst felt by many. Moreover, the fear of the devastations the disease wreaked on the global economy, decreased employment and availability of workers, supply chains, the shutting down of places of entertainment, sports venues, and places of recreation and retreat, all signaled an abrupt and radical change to our way of life. At the same time, the lockdowns and mandates prescribed by government authorities and agencies engendered an equally deep fear that personal liberties and rights were being taken away, a fear that caused many to resist and protest the restrictions that were being placed on us, sometimes with violence. Communication and engagement that held the possibility of collaboration and greater understanding of COVID's threats and potential preventions gave way to polarized politicalization and divisive attacks, with each side blaming the other for something over which no one had much control.

It does not matter what the issue is, whether COVID, global warming, gun violence, racism, economic disparity, or any of the others that we have named, the unregulated fear and threat that come with the perils we face are sending us into a survival mode mentality. The same reactive dynamics that have taken place throughout the pandemic occur over and over again! We attack rather than communicate and embrace, we curse what we perceive to be the bad things happening to us or the bad things we perceive others doing to us. We resent and discredit those who are trying to help us, demanding that we be able to control our own lives with relative or no intervention! It seems to be a truth that when our life is disrupted or we perceive it to be under threat, the undertow of fear takes over and leads us into behaviors and ways of treating each other that have more to do with the powers of death than the culture of life. Fear has led us to be a culture stuck in survival mode.

Fear in Politics, Public Discourse—and Church Life

Consider for a moment how this undercurrent of unregulated fear has changed our political landscape, political conversations and public discourse. There was a time when political leaders could argue and hold legitimate and fiery debates, where elections were intense, but when they were over, they were for the most part over. Political opponents were not necessarily enemies. When conceding defeat to President Bill Clinton, the late Senator Bob Dole said:

> I've said repeatedly in this campaign that the President was my opponent and not my enemy. And I wish him well, and I pledge my support in whatever advances the cause of a better America because that's what the race was about in the first place, a better America as we go into the next century.[5]

As Dole's comments suggest, there was a sense that the common good was far more important than holding political grudges. But, somewhere that changed. For conservatives, the word "liberal" became synonymous with evil, and vice versa for liberals, each viewing the other as a threat and an enemy to be defeated at all costs, even if that cost is democracy itself, our common good, or the bonds that hold us together as a community. Unregulated fear has led to a dehumanization and demonizing of political opponents. It has led to the politics of ideology where adherence to a particular ideology takes precedence over the common good, and where the questioning of that ideology is not allowed, at least for those members of the party who purport the ideology. We are afraid of those who think differently, those who believe differently, and those whose appearance is different. Moreover, the attraction of particular ideologies is that they offer us a kind of certainty about the future; ideologies become unquestioned beliefs because "they are right," an assertion that is true for both the right and the left.

The undercurrent of fear existing in much of our present political discourse has led to another and perhaps even greater danger. It is the danger that comes when human beings are dehumanized because they are perceived to be a threat to our existence. That dehumanization extends beyond political discourse. It extends to our perceptions and treatment of "undesirables" and those who are on the margins of life, especially the extreme margins of life. This demonic spirit of dehumanization is evident and comes into the open in an article by Alexander Zubatov, a New York attorney and author. In that article titled, "We Are Living in the Ruins of our Civilization," Zubatov decried and derided what he observed when taking a night tour of New York City. Referring to a human being who is almost unconscious or dead from alcohol, he says,

> The first higher species of being I come across is only a shadow of any such description—a teetering, drooling zombie barely maintaining the accustomed vertical orientation of humanity—its head, neck, and back doubling over further and further, heavy

---

5. Dole, "Concession Speech," lines 12–16.

Part I: The World We Live In

eyelids drooping down time and again on the remaining vestiges of any consciousness to which it only weakly clings.[6]

Notice the condescending description, "The first higher species . . ." Later, the same condescension occurs when he refers to the behavior he observed in two men he calls "brown bums." Zubatov says that they were "like ungainly insects going through the motions of a mating ritual both know will end in anticlimax."[7] The people he saw and observed were in his eyes not human. They were bums, animals and insects! His indictment of the humanity he observed reveals the pernicious hate that comes in dehumanization.

> I know the unyielding ukase of my educated pedigree and those who share it is that empathy and compassion are the only sanctioned responses to this sorry spectacle. But that would require me to rationalize my way out of a feeling and override all my sound, sane animal instincts. Those instincts are of pre-cognitive repulsion and disgust, and I refuse to let them go. I refuse to humanize those who cannot be bothered to lift a finger to humanize themselves. The mentally ill need our care. The rest need the whip. In the long run, all of us—they most of all—will be thankful for it.[8]

The late Michael Gerson, an opinion editorial writer for the *Washington Post* took note of this article and responded. Aligning Zubatov's comment with much of what he observes in our current political climate, he noted that a significant segment of our population believes and purports our country is "beset by internal threats from migrants, Muslims, multiculturalists, Black Lives Matter activists, antifa militants and various thugs, gangbangers and whiners."[9] It is a political climate fed by fear that has led to the destructive and deadly dehumanization of anyone falling into these categories. More pernicious still is that by definition, the dehumanization of one human being by another means that the one who is dehumanizing the other has taken upon themselves the role of determining the standards by which another, or groups of others, are judged human or inhuman. This is not only dehumanization, it is entitlement and power domination! Usually these entitled judges, like Zubatov, are guided by their precognitive repulsions and disgust, repulsions and disgusts which they refuse to let go.

6. Zubatov, "Ruins," lines 9–13.
7. Zubatov, "Ruin," lines 27–29.
8. Zubatov, "Ruins," lines 19–25.
9. Gerson, "White Grievance," para 5.

In his response to Zubatov's article, Gerson makes a disturbing observation: the largest group of people who make up this lethal climate are people who claim to be evangelical and nationalistic Christians. This is in spite of the fact that the teachings of Jesus have no room or place for dehumanization or the dehumanizing treatment of any other human being, regardless of their condition. Gerson makes the point and bears witness to our Christian faith when he says, "Christians are informed—not by political correctness, but by Jesus—that every addict and homeless person you might encounter on a nocturnal walk in New York is the presence of Christ in disguise." Moreover, he says,

> This Christian anthropology does not dictate specific policies. But it requires Christians to ask: How should we act in the political realm if every human being we encounter—everyone we admire and everyone we disdain; everyone we agree with and everyone we disagree with; everyone we love and everyone we hate—were actually the image of Christ in our midst? No one can live in this manner at every moment. But it is an ideal that should cause us to tremble.[10]

Moore's comments about the dangers of unregulated fear are directly applicable to the fear that exists in our present political and public discourse. It causes us to attack rather than embrace, to dehumanize rather than humanize those who are different or who we have labeled as dangerous threats; it causes us to spend more time focusing on perceived dangers—like immigrants—rather than see opportunities and ways we could help them; it causes us to hang on to angers and resentments and demand control, as Zubatov's frightful image of using the whip on "undesirables," so aptly testifies.

Parallel and related to the disruptions that survival mode and fear based thinking have brought to political and government functioning, they have also affected our ability to have fruitful public and communal discourse around the critical and life threatening issues we face as a human community. Each of the issues named in chapter 1—gun violence, racism and white superiority, economic disparity, climate change and global warming—pose life threatening devastations, yet for some reason, the conversations that surround them are more often than not loaded with defensiveness, resistance, anger, and at times even physical hostility. With

---

10. Gerson, "White Grievance," para 6–7.

so much at stake for so many, what is it about these conversations that make them so difficult or even volatile?

The answer is simple: they are fear-filled, threatening conversations, even if they are intended to be educational and non-threatening. It is quite ironic that for many, these conversations are viewed and experienced as an even larger threat than the issue or devastation being discussed. I return to the illustration given in chapter 1 referencing the anti-racism statement that called on congregations to undertake intentional and serious conversations on racism and white supremacy. As noted, there was considerable reaction to the statement, with one person calling it "a hostile statement," while others truthfully commented on the difficulty they would have bringing it to their congregations, must less getting their congregations to initiate a commitment to the work of anti-racism. As I have already suggested, the piece that evoked the most resistance and defensiveness was its call for individuals to name the disease of racism within themselves and within their congregations. It was the fear of naming—or having it named!—that something is wrong with us, with our congregations, and with our communities! Such naming elicits feelings of guilt and even shame, both of which are repugnant in a culture that is bent on feeling good all the time. We are reminded of Douglas John Hall's comment: Christians in our culture seem resistant to hearing that anything is seriously wrong; rather they go to church seeking a sanctuary where they can hear a word that says everything is right with the world because God is in heaven.[11] This, of course, is in stark contrast to the gospel—and to Luther's theology of the cross—that invites and asks us to name our sin with courageous truthfulness and candor. In a strange and paradoxical way, the gospel calls and invites us to name with specificity those things that feel shameful and even dangerous to bring into the open, precisely because that is the place God meets us to begin the work of healing, restoration, and becoming new!

The fear of naming that something is wrong with us is the same dynamic that is taking place in school board meetings and other venues when the issue of teaching Critical Race Theory is publicly discussed. It's the same dynamic that takes place when issues of gun control, global warming, or the economic disparity between rich and poor are discussed. We do not want to name that something is wrong with us—individually or communally—or that we are responsible for or have contributed to the maladies

---

11. Hall, *Imaging God*, 1.

that exist. Regardless of our religious or faith background, there is a self-righteous illusion that we simply do not want punctured!

Perhaps the most disturbing aspect of survival mode is that it prevents us from hearing the stories and experiences of suffering that are behind every one of these conversations, whether they are about racism, climate change, gun violence, wealth inequity, sexual violence, and so forth. For the family of an addict trying to help their loved one become sober, it is painful enough to have the addict choose to stay in his addiction; but it it is a significantly deep pain to realize that he has not heard your suffering and your deep care for whether or not he lives. It is a deep pain to realize that in his illness and addiction he has isolated himself from you, physically, emotionally, and spiritually. All that matters to him is satisfying his addictive needs! It is the same pain persons of color feel when white people refuse to talk about racism or do anything about it. It is the same pain LGBQT people feel when congregations refuse to talk about inclusion, the same pain felt by the poor when their plight and cries for help are ignored. And that is exactly why life in chronic survival mode is so isolating and non life giving. Unless we are mindful and attuned to the sufferings of our neighbors, there can be no authentic life giving community. Is it any wonder that Jesus continually reminded his followers not to be consumed by fear?

Fear in Congregational Life

Thus far, we have noted how life in survival mode has adversely and dangerously affected our ability to have fruitful and productive political and public discourse on life threatening issues. But life in chronic survival mode is not limited to these domains. It is also adversely affecting the life and mission of many local congregations across denominational lines. While its effects may not be as obvious as in the previous domains discussed, it is no less present in congregations and it is preventing them from living into their vocational call to be a culture of life in their communities. Its presence is manifested in two distinct ways: the first is what I call, "playing it safe;" the second is "when can we get things back to the way they were." We are reminded of Moore's comment:

> In survival mode, you spend so much time focusing on the dangers that you miss out on the opportunities . . . Survival mode shuts off the part of you that takes risks, uses your imagination,

Part I: The World We Live In

and goes with the flow, and instead directs all that precious energy to the part that plays it safe.[12]

This very dynamic is exemplified in the story of Kenneth Wheeler, an ELCA pastor. In a recent article he shared his grief and anger at being pigeon holed by his bishop as a "good Black pastor" when he graduated from seminary, meaning that as a Black pastor he would never be able to serve in a white congregation. He reflects with these words:

> This white pigeonholing of who I am as a Black man in this country and as a Black pastor in the ELCA has persisted. It has limited my movement, my mobility and the kind of congregations I was offered. I would never be afforded the opportunity of having my name considered for call in a white congregation, because, sadly, there would be other bishops who felt the same as the one who greeted me over the phone. I believe that bishop was blinded by racism, as are many who feel they must protect their white congregants—the clearest way for them to do so was never to submit my name to those congregations.[13]

And what, exactly, is it that needs protection in mainstream white congregations? So much so that a Black brother in the faith, one who has accepted God's call and been approved for ordination to serve the church of Jesus Christ, cannot even be considered as a legitimate candidate to serve a white congregation! One wonders if the bishop had preconceived ideas and images of how this pastors's presence would affect the stability of the congregation? Or did he have preconceived ideas that this pastor did not have the skills needed to serve and lead a white congregation, that he was singularly capable of serving and leading only a black congregation? What fear lurked in the not too distant background that caused this bishop to play it safe and not take the risk of recommending a pastor who might stretch the congregation's vision of itself, who might stretch the congregation by bringing a new perspective of what it means to be the church in the world? Was it a fear that such a move would decrease the membership and giving? Whatever his reasons, the bishop exercised his power out of fear, not love! He was concerned to preserve and maintain the stability of the status quo. To put it even more bluntly, the status quo of white congregations meant more to him than what his actions would mean for Wheeler's future. He played it safe in order to help white congregations play it safe.

12. Moore, "Survival Mode," Lines 4–9.
13. Kenneth Wheeler, "Little by Little," 39.

The idea of "protecting mainstream white congregations" is ubiquitous and it extends to other demographics as well. Consider congregations who are afraid of how they will be identified if too many LGBTQ persons come through their doors. Consider congregations who are afraid of having homeless persons sit in their pews for fear of how they will appear or smell. Consider congregations that want to attract a more diverse cultural and ethnic population into their community by providing programs "for" those communities, yet don't want to make the changes to their communal way of life or worship that would truly transform them into a diverse and multicultural congregation. You get the picture. Our communal, corporate, and systemic efforts to protect a particular way of life may provide us an immediate sense of well being and security, but in the long run, they are not life giving at all, for those protecting their way of life and for those who have been excluded. Fear always creates a dangerous isolation!

There is another form of survival mode that is so subtle we may have difficulty recognizing its similarities to those we have just mentioned! It is the survival mode existing in worshiping congregations when present and settled ways of life are severely and abruptly threatened, as has been the case in a pandemic where gathering for worship poses significant health risks. It is the survival mode existing when a congregation's future is threatened by changing demographics and neighborhoods, or diminishing memberships and financial resources. It is a survival mode most commonly expressed and heard in the urgent plea "when will we return things to normal" or "when can we return things to the way they used to be." Consistent with survival mode and fear based thinking, these pleas and attempts are rooted in a high anxiety and grief over what is being lost, an anxiety and grief that is understandable. At the same time, it is an anxiety that prevents an honest and candid appraisal of the predicament as well as a candid assessment of the possibilities and limits of moving forward. More to the point, the posture of these congregations can become like a pair of hands tightly clenched around an object for fear of losing it. The object is so valued, the person holding on to it cannot imagine life without it. When all of the energies are focused on maintaining the tight grip, the ability to devote imagination and energy to alternative ways of having life are significantly diminished. Clenched fists that hold on to something so tightly betray the presence of an enormous fear. That's exactly the danger many congregations face when they perceive themselves in a perilous situation; they tend to form a tight-fisted grasp around whatever it is they are holding on to in such a way that it prevents them from imagining and reaching out to a life beyond what they have known.

A brief vignette will illustrate this. Second Church is a congregation that was at one time a thriving congregation in a suburban setting. It was strong in its missional outreach to the community. Over the past years, the demographics of the congregation have shifted to a growing older population. Likewise the demographics of the community in which it is situated have changed drastically to a racially, culturally, and economically diverse community. The community and the congregation are no longer what they were. Rather than stop to make an honest assessment of their context and changes they might have to make, they instead viewed their problem—like many congregations do—as one that could be solved with an influx of young members who would increase their energy level and financial resources. Like many congregations, the strategy for making that happen was to call a young pastor with energy and creativity, which they did. What didn't change, however, was the congregation's grasp with which it holds on to its past, a grasp that makes it almost impossible to see beyond itself and its narrow vision of the future. As hard as the new young pastor worked to help the congregation open itself to new possibilities, it remains stuck. Moreover, its way of congregational life seems not open to new faces and new ways of thinking, which means that it rarely sees visitors. Without even knowing it, the grasp with which they are holding on to their past has dangerously isolated them, not just from the community around them, but from possibilities that might offer them new life and energy.

Whether in our political climate, our public discourse, or the world of our congregational life, the undercurrent of fear is strong and fierce. It is what keeps us living in chronic survival mode. When survival mode becomes a sustained, anxious way of life that seeks to preserve status, privilege, or power, or when it seeks to return things to normal and revive a past that is no longer possible, it paradoxically brings emotional, spiritual and even physical death. For individuals, life in chronic survival mode adversely affects the body, physically, spiritually and emotionally. It adversely affects relationships simply because the individual cannot focus on anyone or anyone's needs beyond one's self. What is true for individuals is also true for governments, communities, groups, and organizations, and as we have seen, organizations like Christian congregations. Energies become so focused on the immediate matters of saving normalcy or the past that the organization or church community cannot see beyond itself.

More devastating is the fact that their ability to live into a life giving future is diminished!

The Idolatry of Survival Mode

Two saying of Jesus are pertinent to our discussion. The first is from his Sermon on the Mount, recorded in Matthew: "For where your treasure is, there will your heart be also."[14] The second is also recorded in Matthew: ". . . if any want to become my followers, let them deny themselves and take up their cross and follow me. For those who want to save their own life will lose it, and those who lose their life for my sake will find it."[15] When our heart is set on holding on to something or a way of life with the belief that without it we cannot have life, whatever it is we are grasping has become our idolatrous god! In his explanation to the first commandment, Luther said,

> God is that to which we are to look for all good and in which we are to find refuge in all need. Therefore to have a god is nothing else than to trust and believe in that one with your whole heart. As I have often said, it is the trust and faith of the heart alone that make both God and idol.[16]

A survival mode of existence is idolatrous precisely for this reason: our hearts have placed their trust and faith in specific and particular ways of life as the ultimate source of refuge, security, and well being, and in turn our life spirits and energies are devoted to preserving them at all costs. In giving them our life energies, we actually worship them. But that's exactly what idolatry does: it keeps us tied and attached to something that cannot give life; it keeps us in the illusion and delusion that if we work hard enough at holding on to whatever that thing is, we will find what we are looking for. Survival mode leads us to believe we can control things over which we are not likely to have much control. In the meantime, weariness sets in, our spirits and energies are depleted, and we can no longer become or live into our call to be a culture of life in the face of death.

Another way to speak of this inward turn is to call it what it is—narcissistic self-absorption. This narcissistic self-absorption is precisely what Luther saw in his own time, particularly as it related to monastic attempts

---

14. Matt 6:21, NRSV.
15. Matt 16: 24–25, NRSV.
16. *TLC*, 300.

at laying hold of God and the security of eternal life through its intense and rigorous practices. These practices were rooted in a deep seated fear of God's wrath and an eternity spent in the fires of hell, all of which created a physical, emotional, and spiritual self-absorption focused on fulfilling the obligations of those practices to avoid such terrifying judgment. But he also saw this same self-absorption in the laity—and the church's exploitation of it—in their attempts to lay hold of God and eternal life through the purchasing of indulgences and other means through which eternal security could be guaranteed. For the laity, the fear that motivated their self-absorption was the same as the monastics, a fear of God's wrath and eternity spent in hell. They lived with a chronic fear of being judged unworthy, a fear that turned them inward to rely on their own efforts to become good enough.

Ours is a very different culture separated by centuries from Medieval and Reformation cultures. In spite of this time span, our similarities are astounding. Albeit in very different ways, we, too, are a culture that is narcissistically self-absorbed. And just like the medieval and Reformation cultures, our self-absorption is driven by an unregulated fear of being judged unworthy, never good enough, or never having enough. It does not matter who or what the gods are that create the codes by which these determinations are made. In the psyche, soul, and spirit of our culture, they are real and they have created the deep and abiding fear of never being good enough or never having enough. It is a fear that has led to a self-absorbed way of life that keeps us living in chronic survival mode at the expense of living out the vocational purposes for which we were created! We see its presence in those obsessed with the protection of their status, privilege, and power at the expense of those for whom their indulgence denies the basic necessities of life. We see it in our culture's indulgence on goods and products that deplete the earth's resources, damage the air we breathe, the water we need for life, and the land that feeds us. We see it in our endless pursuit of commodities that will improve our bodies, our physical appearances, and even increase our sexual gratification. Paradoxically, the things we seek to satisfy our appetites really never satisfy anything. They only create the desire for more. The insecurities we seek to overcome actually remain and grow more intense.

In our culture, the danger of idolatrous self-absorption is the sense of entitlement and privilege to which it eventually leads. It becomes even more dangerous when that entitlement and privilege are undergirded by the belief that an individual or group has earned and is deserving of them by virtue of their race, religion, or status in society. It is a self-absorption that has led to violence, hostility, and brutal death. It is a self-absorbed narcissism that makes an enemy out of anyone who does not agree with a prescribed way of thinking, or anyone who is perceived to be a threat to their entitled way of life. Moreover, it is a self-absorption that leads one to believe that they must take matters into their own hands if they are to find any hope of "stopping the enemy." I suggest that it is this sense of entitlement that led to the brutal deaths of Ahmaud Arbery, and others. It is this sense of entitlement that led to the January 6, 2020, insurrection on the U.S. Capitol and continues to harbor a belief that violence must be used if America is to be restored.

Regardless of the form it takes, and regardless of whether it results in incidents of violence and death or indulgence and consumerism that deplete resources and deny the necessities of life to others, narcissistic self-absorption by its very nature can never be life giving. It is a survival mentality and mode of living that will always lead to death, whether physically, spiritually, or emotionally.

Privatizing the Faith—A Theology of Glory

The behaviors we have described and illustrated in this discussion, particularly as they relate to Christians, are undergirded by a prevailing theology and belief about God, about who God is in the world, about who God is in relationship to human beings, and about who human beings are in relationship to God. Given this, it behooves us to look with a critical eye at what sort of theology and belief system gives rise to and undergirds this survival mode of existence.

Each and every incident or behavior that was noted in the previous section is a vivid example of narcissistic self-absorption. Persons concerned with preserving and protecting their individual privileges over the welfare and health of the community are self-absorbed. A nation or groups within a nation who want to resurrect a past and culture that protects their particular way of life and seeing the world, but excludes others or pays no attention to their needs, cares and concerns, are narcissistically self-absorbed. Harsh as it may sound, congregations focused on resurrecting a past or returning things to normal at the expense of hearing the sufferings in their neighborhoods or communities are narcissistically self-absorbed. The bottom line is that any individual or group that sets out to save and protect itself for the sake of itself is narcissistically self-absorbed. Nothing else matters but itself; its life and life energies are devoted only to itself!

Already in 1978, Christopher Lasch, the American historian, social critic, and former professor at the University of Rochester, saw this self-absorbed culture emerging when he wrote his book, *The Culture of Narcissism*. He observed and noted that our self-absorbed obsession with pursuing endless happiness, comfort, and self-gratification is in fact a facade and cover up for the brokenness and despair that is felt deep within. Our narcissistic self-absorption is in reality a search for deeper levels of hope, meaning and purpose, perverted though those searches can become. He profoundly and accurately comments that this pervasive obsession with the self is rooted "in the subjective experience of emptiness and isolation." The things and movements to which we attach ourselves with the hope of finding salvation, are in fact, Lasch observes, attempts at repudiating "a profound despair and resignation. It is the faith of those without faith."[17]

"The faith of those without faith" is, in fact, a theology of glory. As we have already seen, a theology of glory is a way of life that is expressed in the self's belief, trust, and confidence in itself to give life to itself. It seeks to have and hold on to life for its own purposes. It is a way of life that seeks its refuge, security and well being through its own pursuits. It is a way of life for which the normal sufferings, pains and vulnerabilities of life are repugnant and are to be avoided. It is a way of life based on pretense and illusion.

When Luther spoke of a theology of glory he was referring to a way of life that is so turned into self and self-absorbed it cannot see beyond itself to see the needs of neighbor or the effects its self-absorption is having on others. He states this rather clearly in his explanation to the first commandment pertaining to the worship of other gods.

> There are some who think they have God and everything they need when they have money and property; they trust in them and boast in them so stubbornly and securely that they care for no one else.[18]

He goes on to say that the self "is unwilling to receive anything as a gift of God," but desires "to earn everything by itself or to merit everything by works . . ." Moreover, the self looks upon God as though "God were in our service or debt and we were God's liege lords." Luther names this idolatry! "What is this but to have made God into an idol . . . and to have set

---

17. Lasch, *Culture of Narcissism*, 51.
18. *TLC*, 301.

ourselves up as God."[19] Nothing could more aptly describe the religion of our narcissistic culture of self-absorption, self-centeredness, and its theology of glory: we think God is there to reward us for our hard work and to give us the things to which we feel entitled because we have earned and deserved them! We are gods, and God exists to serve us.

Douglas John Hall aptly calls this "a warped imagining of the self."[20] From his point of view, the problems that have resulted from self-absorbed narcissism—like economic orders that benefit the wealthy but marginalize the poor—will not fully be rectified by mere problem solving or even a redistribution of wealth. Hall rather bluntly cuts to the heart of the matter when he says, "the problem is not a matter of having or doing; it is a matter of being." He goes on with poignant and prophetic words that help us grasp the gravity of what Luther meant when he talked about the idolatrous abuse of God and having set ourselves up as God. Hall suggests that the root and foundational fact underlying our economic disparities is

> that our First World patterns of lifestyle and possession emerge out of a profoundly entrenched image of who we are. It is our being-who-we-are that constitutes the problem. We resent this message deeply when it is proclaimed to us by the victims of our high self image. But no signifiant changes in the arrangement of the world will occur until we ourselves have felt the truth of this judgment . . . What is wrong with us is wrong at the level of our being as such—not, of course that we exist but the manner in which we body forth our existence . . . For the changes that are requisite for planetary survival and shalom are not surface rearrangements like the redistribution of the material goods and services, but a transformation at the level of personal and social being. In short, we must get a new image of ourselves; we ourselves must be changed![21]

Narcissistic self-absorption is the cultural food we have been fed from birth. Following the old adage that "we are what we eat," we have eaten a food that has warped us and turned us into self-absorbed human beings. But, as Hall observes, ". . . nothing has been as influential in the creation of images of the human, historically speaking, as religion."[22] Think about this for a moment. If our country is a "Christian nation,"—as the Christian

---

19. *TLC*, 303.
20. Hall, *Imaging God*, 11.
21. Hall, *Imaging God*, 13.
22. Hall, *Imaging God*, 14.

nationalist movement and others so loudly purport—then how do we explain that "the worship of the Christian God is related to our being this kind of society," that is, a narcissistically self-absorbed culture. Furthermore, "Are we to conclude that Christianity itself has given birth to a society whose citizenry can be nonchalant about the fact that it, a small fraction of the planet's human occupancy can lay claim to almost half of its neutral resources?"[23] Hall rightly observes that what might be wrong with us is that we misunderstand what the Christian faith is about and what it is calling us to be. More deeply, he suggests, the real problem is in our conception and image of who God is. In our self-absorbed narcissism, we believe God exists to satisfy our desires and appetites. It is this belief that has warped our imaging of ourselves.

Aligning with Hall's observation, I suggest that the problem with our conceptions and images of God is that our self-absorbed narcissism has led us to deeply internalize the belief that how I believe or what I do with God is a private matter. Such privatizing of faith and our relationship with God means that we are able to keep God out of the public realm and isolated from the critical issues that are threatening our lives.

Louise Kretzschmar, ethicist and systematic theologian who teaches at the University of South Africa, defined the privatization of the Christian faith to mean "the limitation of the Gospel to the private, spiritual concerns of the individual."[24] She used this term in reference to what she observed of her own denomination, the Baptist Union of South Africa, during that country's struggles with apartheid. In her thesis written in 1992, she argued "that the Baptist Union of South Africa understood and practiced the Christian faith in a privatized fashion. They failed fully to identify or proclaim the social content and implications of the Christian faith and they subscribed to a diluted Gospel."[25] In our context, that is exactly what has happened. Living in chronic survival mode, we have retreated into the comfort of a diluted gospel that spiritualizes and privatizes its message, yet fails and refuses to heed its warning that there are dire consequences if the cries and groans of the suffering, the hungry, the oppressed and the poor are not heard and attended to.

As Kretzschmar points out, salvation is considered a personal matter that is restricted to "getting things right with God;" reconciliation has to do

23. Hall, *Imaging God*, 15.
24. Kretzschmar, "Privatization," 128.
25. Kretzschmar, "Privatization," 128.

with personal relationships, but little to do with the broader reconciliation between peoples or the earth when it comes to exploitation, discrimination, injustice, or dehumanization, a reconciliation to which the gospel explicitly call us![26] When the practice of the privatization of the gospel restricts its message to a personalized view of salvation that excludes the gospel's distinct call for justice and reconciliation, that practice thereby, wittingly or unwittingly, promotes an active disengagement from the very human struggles and sufferings in which most human beings in the world find themselves. There is nothing at all wrong with the notion and view that salvation has to do with one's personal relationship with God. It is part and parcel of the gospel! But as Kretzschmar accurately notes, when faith is allowed to stop there or intentionally prohibited from going any further, the broader and more holistic message of the gospel that calls us into a new way of life of actively standing in solidarity with the poor, the hungry, the marginalized and oppressed is completely missed.[27] In missing that message and life, we can go through the rituals and motions of our faith without much change to anything.

While the word and language of privatization normally refers to the transfer of assets and operations from government to the private sector, it is an important word and concept to the world of God and faith. In the world of economics and finance, it specifically means that the "control" of whatever it is that is being transferred is now under the control of private hands rather than public or governmental hands. I suggest it has a similar meaning when we use it with reference to our faith. For when faith is privatized, it as though I am now in control of it and how it directs my life rather than the other way around. When I am in control, my faith no longer asks me questions or challenges the directions I am choosing for my life. It only gives me certainty, because that's what I choose! I choose what meaning God has for my life, how I will worship God, if I choose to worship at all. I choose how it will shape my identity as a human being. Just as the privatization of property allows me to determine how my property will be used, the privatization of God and faith means that I determine how I will "use" them rather than opening myself to the meanings, directions, and purposes to which they will lead me even if those directions, meanings, and purposes are not "pleasing" to me. In short, privatization means that God

---

26. Kretzschmar, "Privatization," 130.
27. Kretzschmar, "Privatization," 131.

and faith are like commodities from which I can pick and choose, depending on which ones I feel "fit" my life or will improve it!

Perhaps the most adverse effect of the privatization of God and faith is that it opens the door for me to be the one who decides the nature and gravity of my sinfulness, or whether or not sin is even a part of my being. In effect, privatization means that I become my own judge. Since God and faith are now private matters, I am the one who determines what voices I listen to or not listen to when it comes to making judgment on the nature and gravity of my sin, or making judgment on what change is required of me to live in reconciliation with God. Does it come as any surprise to discover that when it comes to confessing and repenting of our sin, we will generally play it safe? That is, we confess and repent of those things that will not cause much upheaval or disruption to our life. Privatizing God and the faith means that we can make confession, yet feel safe and secure in our status quo! Nothing much has to change! Another way to put it is that when God and faith are privatized, we run the high risk of taking God for granted, as the psalmist describes in Psalm 50 where he has God speaking:

> For you hate discipline and you cast my words behind you.
> You make friends with a thief when you see one,
> and you keep company with adulterers.
> You give your mouth free rein for evil, and your tongue frames deceit,
> You speak against your kin; you slander your own mother's child.
> These thing you have done and I have been silent;
> You thought that I was one just like yourself.[28]

When a government operation is privatized and transferred to private ownership, the new owner works to reduce as much government interference as possible. That's exactly what happens when God and faith are privatized. We don't want anyone telling us about our sins; we don't want anyone calling us to accountability, telling us what is wrong with us or what we need to change. We are reminded of Hall's observation that Christians seem content not to hear that anything is seriously wrong, but instead go to church to hear the palliative and comforting word that all is right with God and the world. Is it any wonder that preachers get into trouble when they speak to the gospel's call to practice justice in the public realm? When our privatized faith and concepts of God are punctured, and when we are prophetically told that we are accountable to something beyond ourselves, we vehemently react and push back.

28. Ps 50: 16–21, NRSV.

Life in Survival Mode

While the privatization of God and the faith may satisfy our immediate and self-absorbed narcissistic appetites for personal security and well being, it eventually leads to death, whether physically, spiritually, or emotionally. It does so precisely because privatization leads us into isolation from the communal nature of life that God intendeds for all of creation. We are reminded of what Paul says when he references the body in the twelfth chapter of First Corinthians: no part of the body can isolate itself from any other part of the body. If one part of the body considers itself more important than the other, or if it tries to isolate itself, the body cannot function as it is intended.[29] Extending Paul's analogy, we can also say that when a Christian congregation turns itself inward and focuses only on its privatized survival, it ceases to function, live, and serve the vocational purposes for which Christ is calling it into being.

Hall is right. The theological problem that undergirds our misguided survival mode of existence is a gross misunderstanding and distortion of who God is in the world and who we are in relationship to God. Moreover, it is a gross distortion of the gospel and what that gospel is calling us to be as the body of Christ in the world. To use Luther's language, we have distorted the gospel into a theology of glory, a theology of self-preservation and triumphalism. But the gospel is not a privatized faith that has to do only with God, me, my personal reconciliation with God, or my personal triumphs. It is a public and communal faith that has everything to do with the reconciliation of all people to God, to each other, and to all of creation; it has to do with seeing and responding to the Christ who meets us in each and every human being that enters our life, regardless of how they appear or smell! It is a faith that beckons us to leave old survival modes of existence to become and live into the newness of a culture of life. It is a life that exists in the grasp of God's near, persistent, and eternal love, and it is a life that resists death's devastations, even as their dangers are growing.

---

29. 1 Cor 12:14–26, NRSV.

3

The Empowering but Unsettling Hope of the Gospel

Led Into Unknowing and Awakened to New Becoming—The Work of the Spirit

LEAVING SURVIVAL MODES OF existence to become and live into a culture of life—the kingdom of God—is not easy. In fact, Luther is clear: it is not a work we do of our own accord. It is God who does this work, a work Luther asserts and affirms in his instruction on the third article of the creed, "I believe in the Holy Spirit, the Holy catholic church, the communion of saints, the forgiveness of sins, the resurrection of the body, and the life everlasting." For Luther, this confession is significantly more than a statement about the nature and mysteries of the Holy Spirit. Like the first and second articles, it is a statement about the work God does and the realities God creates in bringing forth life. In this instance, it is about the life giving work God does in the third person of the Trinity, the life giving work Luther calls "being made holy."

> To this article, as I have said, I cannot give a better title than "Being Made Holy." In it are expressed and portrayed the Holy Spirit and her office, which is that the Spirit makes us holy . . . As the First Person of the Trinity is called a Creator and the Son is called

a Redeemer, so on account of her work, the Holy Spirit must be called a Sanctifier, one who makes us holy.[1]

One way to think about this sanctifying work—this work of being made holy—is to think of it as transformative work; it is the Spirit's work that is transforming us into something we are yet to be. It is the work and action of the Spirit which Luther understood to take place within the community of the church, the communion of saints within which the forgiveness of sins is a practice and mark of its life together, along with its faith, trust, and hope in God's future. He puts it this way: "... the Spirit first leads us into the holy community, places us in the church's lap, where the Spirit preaches to us and brings us to Christ."[2] Stjerna observes that in this simple sentence, "... Luther points to the reality of the church, not as a building or an institution, essentially, but as action: where the word is proclaimed and where the word acts, there the Spirit works—and that is church."[3] What Stjerna's observation explicitly declares is *that church is not a noun; it is a verb!* Think about that! Yes, church happens wherever the Word is spoken, proclaimed, and offered in the sacraments; yet at the very same time, church happens where that word acts upon those who hear it in such a way so as empower and transform them into communities who themselves will become transforming agents in the world, agents of forgiveness, reconciliation, justice, and hope! In the context of our discussion, church is the action of the Spirit that transforms us from survival modes of existence into our holy vocation of becoming a culture of life in the face of death's powers.

An analogy that can help understand this concept of church as action is the culture that evolves when water and flour are mixed together. As any baker knows, when those two elements are brought together and allowed to sit with each other, the natural yeasts in the flour activate and a culture begins to form. This culture will eventually grow into a starter that will then have the agency and power to transform the ingredients of flour and water into loaves of bread. Note that as this culture forms, the flour and water are changed into a totally new substance from what they were, a substance that itself will then have transformative agency when it is mixed with other ingredients. Note, also, that neither the flour nor the water do anything to effect the action that is taking place. They are acted upon, and in being acted upon they become something other than what they have been and

1. *TLC*, 358–59.
2. *TLC*, 360.
3. *TLC*, 360.

they now have a transforming agency that they did not have. *The culture that has been formed is no longer a noun; it is now a verb; it is action that is constantly occurring and an action that needs constant nurturing in order to be sustained!* From my perspective, this analogy helps us understand what Luther meant when he talked about the office of the Spirit as being the work of making us holy! To be made holy is to be transformed into a culture of life, a culture that will itself have transformative agency in the face of the powers of death.

To be sure, the analogy of a sourdough culture will have its limits. Its association with the pleasant and calming aromas of bread baking do not make it sound like an analogy that would speak to unsettled disruption. The truth is, however, that the emergence of a culture does not come without change, and change will always be unsettling and disruptive, even with inanimate substances like flour and water. Observe the fomenting that takes place as the fermenting action of yeast begins its work. Things get stirred up and they are unsettled; at times, the unsettledness of things can smell repugnant. What I am suggesting is that if, as Stjerna suggests, the church is the action of the Spirit at work in the community of saints, then we can expect nothing less than that it will be empowering, yet unsettling and disruptive to what is comfortable and settled. Nothing stays the same when the Spirit is acting! In our culture of self-absorbed narcissism this is a dis-ease to which we are averse.

The unsettled disruption and dis-ease that comes with change and leaving what is old for what is new is not something we readily expect or identify as the work of the Spirit. Yet if we are to hear and respond to the gospel's radical call to leave survival for vocation, we cannot avoid it. Moreover, Luther's instruction in the *Large Catechism*, particularly his comments on the pilgrimage of baptism, will not allow us to avoid it! Like the culture of a sourdough starter, we must be ready for the fact that to be acted upon by the Spirit will mean substantive changes to our lives, individually and communally, changes that will be unsettling and disruptive to our settled survival modes of existence, yet changes that will be empowering and transformative.

A Word About Vocation

As an ACPE Clinical Educator, I've had the opportunity to work with students who in some form or fashion are working to discover and live into their vocation. The vocation into which they are finding their way is the vocation of ministry, sometimes ministry as parish pastors, and sometimes as a hospital chaplain or a pastoral clinical educator. A common theme for just about all of these candidates is that they begin their work thinking that they have to transcend their humanness, their vulnerabilities, their weaknesses, their family history, or whatever it is that has brought insecurity into their life. Somehow they have an image that they are not adequate and must overcome whatever those things are that leave them feeling as though they can't measure up or won't ever be good enough. Yet along the way, they discover that the things they may have perceived as their greatest weaknesses and vulnerabilities turn out to be their greatest strengths—not because they somehow overcame them or even changed them, but because thy learned to use them differently. It's a very strange paradox, and one that I think has applicability to our discussion about stepping into unknowing and uncertainty, and awakening to new becomings.

The paradox is simply this. Becoming who we are yet to be means stopping the never ending treadmill of trying to outrun the demons that shame and tell us we are inadequate, the demons that tell us we must overcome ourselves and make ourselves into something different if we are to live into the vocational purposes for which we were created. This will sound contradictory and confusing, but it is the truth of the paradox of grace. We can only become the authentic human beings we were created to be when we quit trying to transcend ourselves and allow ourselves to sit in God's transforming grace and be acted upon by the Spirit.

I share a personal story about stepping into such a venture. At first glance it may seem a story that doesn't have much relevance to the global issues we have referenced in this discussion. Yet I trust the reader will see its application. It is a story that took place in my relationship with a clinical pastoral education student who was in the process of becoming an ACPE Certified Educator. Allison (not her real name) is an African American woman who came to her learning pilgrimage with a history of high achievement. She was a hard worker who was anxious to prove herself capable. In fact much of her identity, self-worth, and value was based on proving herself worthwhile through her high achievement. Striving hard to prove herself was the settled way of life she knew. It was her survival mode of existence, especially as an African American woman in a white man's world.

One of the important elements of clinical pastoral education, particularly for someone wanting to become a certified educator, is to have an awareness of one's life history and how that history and all of its relationships have shaped their personal and professional identity. Very quickly, I realized how hard Allison worked to avoid talking about her life story, and in particular, how much she avoided talking about her past experiences and identity as an African American woman. All she could think about was moving forward to achieve what she needed to achieve. She wanted nothing to do with the vulnerabilities of her life or the pain she had experienced. She worked hard to transcend and overcome that story, thinking it was her liability.

Thinking that I needed to "help" her get through her resistance, so as to go to those places, I began to push, and at times confront and challenge her about why she was resisting delving into life history and story. However, true to theories of resistance, the harder I pushed the more Allison resisted. One day, though, she ventured into what for her was an unknown, fear-filled, and very vulnerable place: she took the enormous risk of confronting and challenging me. She looked me in the eye and said, "Wayne, you are an older white man. Do you know my history with older white men who have been my bosses?" Of course I didn't, and of course, I didn't recognize that I might be like all those white men who preceded me. And then she told me.

As I listened to Allison's story and what she was telling me about her history, I was likewise thrown into a vulnerable place: I was being confronted with the truth that I was not who I thought I was. I was just like all the other white males who had been in positions of power in Allison's life. In this moment, however, I was no longer in the position of power, in the position of being the one who was supposed to have the answers or who was supposed to know what she needed to do. Allison was teaching me, and what she was teaching me was an unsettling and disquieting truth about myself. Just as Allison took the risk of becoming vulnerable with me, I now had to take the risk of becoming vulnerable with her. I listened. It was more than a mere listening to words. I listened and heard the pain she had long felt, a pain of which I was not mindful when I maintained a position of power and thought it my job to tell her what she needed to know and do.

As unsettling and disquieting as Allison's words were to me, an awakening was taking place. I was being acted upon! What she told and shared with me awakened me to the fact that there were a whole hosts of racial and paternalistic dynamics present in the room and in our interaction, dynamics of which I was not mindful. In her willingness to venture into the unknown place of making herself vulnerable and sharing her story with me, we both were awakened. As much as I thought of myself as a non-racist and non-paternalistic white male, I was awakened to the truth and reality that I was doing the very same thing all her previous white male bosses and supervisors had done. Like them, I had placed myself in a top-down relationship where I knew what she needed to do and was telling her how to do it. In this moment of unknowing and vulnerability, a profound moment of coming to know was beginning to take place, not because I learned something *about* racism or paternalism; it was profound because I was *awakened to know truths and realities of racism and paternalism as they existed and were being manifested in me, my behavior, and how I was relating to her.*

In that awakening and coming to know, things began to change—for me and for her. What happened is that we both experienced an encounter! I was encountered by Allison and her feelings towards me and what I represented. She was encountered by her own history and story, and by the reality that she could no longer run away from them. They were part of her very being. We were both encountered by things that were "other" in our life, things of which we were unaware or had kept out of our consciousness. They were encounters that awakened us to new possibilities, not only in our educational relationship, but in our vocational directions.

For my part, I worked to change my position as a teacher. Rather than tell her what she needed to do, I moved to become more of a partner with her in her learning pilgrimage, to give her space for determining what she needed to learn and do to progress in her educational process. I learned to trust her. For Allison, her willingness to be vulnerable with her anger and pain awakened her to her own power as a learner, not to mention to a new way of learning. And just as significant, she was surprisingly awakened to an awareness that all of the things in her life story that had caused her fear and distrust, things she had been working so hard to overcome, deny, or hide, did not have the power she thought they did. In fact, she began to realize that however painful her story had been it was still her story and it did not have to be a source of shame. Rather this awakening initiated a pilgrimage of becoming in which she began to use her own story as a powerful resource for how she could relate to people in the same kind of life experience and pain. For both of us, it marked a transition into becoming who we were yet to be by sitting with grace in who we had been and who we were. It sparked a transition in which we both began to learn how to use ourselves and our humanness differently. It was a pilgrimage that began as each of us was encountered and acted upon by the "otherness" of the other.

Part I: The World We Live In

Encountering the "Other"

The gospel's radical call on our life—the work and action of the Spirit—is an encounter with a Word that is "other" an beyond us, "other" and beyond what is familiar and settled in our life; it is an encounter that calls and leads us to leave old, familiar survival modes of existence to become something new and different. That something new and different is a life of vocation summed up in Jesus' words, "You shall love your neighbor as yourself."[4] This is not a call to a new kind of charity. It is a radical call that reaches deep into the heart and core of what it means to be a human being in relationship with every other human being. It is a call that asks us to leave our unregulated fear, anxiety, and self-protected lives to embrace a life of freedom that empowers us to live into a very different relationship with ourselves, our neighbor, the world, and all of creation. As the story of Allison and me attests, this leaving of fear driven lives does not happen until we embrace the space and grace God gives us to sit with who we have been and acknowledge the power that we have given fear to drive our lives. Only when we acknowledge and name it can change and transformation begin. Only then can our encounters with the "otherness" of others lead us into change and a leaving of what is old for what is new. As with much of the gospel's message, it sounds easy enough, except we know it isn't.

The words of Michael Gerson remind us of just how radical this gospel's call really is. "Christians are informed—not by political correctness, but by Jesus—that every addict and homeless person you might encounter on a nocturnal walk in New York is the presence of Christ in disguise."[5] This gospel's good news "requires every Christian to ask how we should act, if every human being we encounter—everyone we admire and everyone we disdain; everyone we agree with and everyone we disagree with; everyone we love and everyone we hate—were actually the image of Christ in our midst?[6] In other words, the good news of the gospel calls us to put on a very different lens through which to see ourselves and every human being that we encounter, regardless of how alike, different, repulsive, or "other" they may be. That's what it means to leave survival for vocation. If it sounds disrupting and disorienting, that's because it is. It is the empowering but unsettling hope of the gospel.

4. Matt 22:39; Mark 12:31, NRSV.
5. Gerson, "White Grievance," para 5.
6. Gerson, "White Grievance," para 5.

The Empowering but Unsettling Hope of the Gospel

Unregulated fear's grasp on our life is strong and oppressive, especially in these perilous and threatening times. With such a grasp on us, how can we even begin to think about following a gospel that calls us to be encountered by peoples and realities that are different and "other" from what we know? But that's the point of the entire gospel—and Luther's instruction. We are not asked to have perfection or be completed products! We are not asked to have perfection as we are encountered by the gospel's "otherness," or the "otherness" of those who are different from ourselves. We are simply asked to open ourselves to what encounters us and to enter into the pilgrimage of new becoming to which that encounter will lead—a pilgrimage that is a life of becoming what we are yet to be. It is a pilgrimage instigated by the Spirit. And make no mistake, this pilgrimage of becoming will always be a life of *living in between.* In becoming what we are yet to be, we will always live between *death and life, darkness and light, sorrow and joy, despair and hope, fear and love, between self-centered narcissism and life giving vocation.*

If leaving survival modes of existence for the vocational life of loving one's neighbor as one's self means anything at all, it means stepping into places of unknowing and uncertainty where we are encountered by peoples, cultures, and realities that are "other" than ourselves and "other" from what we have known and are familiar. It is in these places of "otherness" where we are encountered by the Spirit and the gospel's radical news of God's reconciliation in Jesus the Christ, a reconciliation that is not just with us as private individuals, but with the entire human community and all of creation. It is in these in between places of "otherness" that we are awakened to new beginnings, new beginnings, and new vocational callings.

Javier Alanís, a well known and respected Latiné scholar and teacher, provides a perspective of what this in between existence looks like from the social location of a Hispanic/Latiné/Mestizo/Hybrid person living on the U.S.-Mexican Borderlands. It is a perspective from which those of us whose faith and faith expressions are socially located in white affluent America have much to learn as we navigate the pilgrimage of leaving survival for vocation.

Alanís defines this in between existence as a place of liminality. It is a transitional place where one stands on the threshold of an encounter—an Encuentro. It is the place of new awareness and new consciousness. Liminality defines a Christian's existence in the world, for in truth, we live in two different realms at the same time. As we live, move, and have our being in this world amid its many powers, we are at the very same time situated and living in God's kingdom, awaiting the fulfillment of God's promised future. Both make claims on our lives, and we are always situated in between those claims. On the one hand, the power of the world make claims with which we are familiar; they are our norm. On the other hand, the kingdom of God breaks into our life with a very different set of claims, claims that are distinctly "other" than what we know and with which we are familiar. For Alanís, it is into this liminal third space—this in between place of "otherness"—that we are propelled when we are encountered by the Spirit and the gospel's radical good news.[7]

In this regard, Alanís looks to Phillip's preaching in Samaria[8] as an illustration of the gospel's power in a place of "otherness." He puts it his way:

> Samaria is the place of "otherness," of racial mixture of Jews and Gentiles dating back to the conquest by Assyria. It's the place where "mestizos" dwell, folks of a "hybrid mixture" who become the "Third Other" by conquest and subaltern identity. We have our own Samaria in the Southwest borderlands where mixtures of ethnicities, cultures, languages, theologies, genders and geo-political "Otherness" marks the Latiné community of the many Americas as "perpetual other." These are folks who live on the margins of the powerful empire, on the edges of the church and in the shadows of our communities. We have heard Felipe preaching "the good news" of God's acceptance of our "otherness" in our Samaritan borderland wilderness. We affirm with theological confidence: "El nos conoce muy bien!"—He knows us![9]

In this in between space of "otherness," the good news of the gospel preached by Phillip is that the reconciliation of God in Jesus Christ transcends all cultural, ethnic, gender, geo-political, and linguistic borders of difference. In our baptism, the gospel affirms that all are created in the image and likeness of the creator—*imago Dei*—and in our faith traditions we affirm our God-given dignity! The gospel is hospitality to all who sit and stand in this place of "otherness."[10] To enter into this in between space of "otherness" is to enter into a very different kind of human community. It is this community of "otherness" that we enter when we embark on the pilgrimage

---

7. Alanis, "Third Spaces," slide 4.
8. Acts 8:4–8, NRSV.
9. Alanis, "Third Spaces," slide 7.
10. Alanis, "Third Spaces," slide 12.

of leaving survival for vocation. Leaving what is old for what is new and "other" is never easy. Yet it is in this place of "otherness" as Phillip's preaching testifies that the power of the Spirit and the gospel is made known.

What I am suggesting is that when we leave our settled worlds that are driven by unregulated fear and anxiety and step into our baptismal pilgrimage towards vocation, we are stepping into a liminal and in between space. In some ways it is like stepping into a borderland experience. No, it is not the same as those who have traversed the perils of border crossings, nor is it necessarily the same as those who live in a geographical borderland existence. Yet, it is a borderland experience because we stand in that liminal place where we experience the very existential tensions of being citizens of the world yet citizens of God's kingdom. Sometimes we don't know who we are or where we are standing. It is a borderland experience because we are situated between two identities—a people who have been defined by our culture's self-absorbed and self-protective narcissism and at the same time, a people who have been given a new identity and vision of what it means to be fully and authentically human. And once again, sometimes we don't know which identity we wear or what vision is guiding us. It is a borderland experience because we enter a space, a holy space, where we encounter a holy Spirit every time we are engaged by people and nations who are different and other than ourselves. It is a borderland experience because we live in what is now but not yet; it is a place of ambiguity yet a place of new beginnings, new becomings, and new vocational callings.

But, as Alanís points out, it is in this in between place of "otherness" that the power of the Spirit and the gospel brings forth life. It is in this in between place where the Spirit and the gospel seeds a culture of life that opens the door to new possibilities and new beginnings in the face of perils and threats. In fact, it is in this in between place of "otherness" where we risk being transformed into people who are "other" than what we have been and "other" than a people whose identity is shaped and formed by self-absorbed narcissism and self-protective survival modes of living.

The Call of the Disciples—A Step Into the "Otherness" of Borderland Reality

Borderland reality provides a different but helpful lens through which we might understand the story of Jesus' call of the disciples to follow him. We know the story. As Matthew tells it, Jesus' mission to proclaim the good news, "Repent for the kingdom of heaven has come near,"[11] has just been announced. After this is announced, Matthew tells us that Jesus is walking by the sea where he sees Peter and Andrew, fishers who are attending their nets. There is no drama; Jesus simply says, "Follow me, and I will make you fish for people." No questions are asked about what Jesus meant, nor were questions asked about what following Jesus would mean for their life. They simply followed. The same call is issued again when Jesus sees James and John. He calls and they immediately follow with no questions asked. In following Jesus, the disciples step into the liminal space between the world they have known and an unknown future to which they have been called, a borderland reality, if you will. It is the liminal and in between space in which they are encountered and acted upon by the "otherness" of Jesus and the transforming power of the gospel.

As difficult as their fishing life was, particularly under the Roman imperial rules that governed the fishing industry,[12] it was still the settled life they knew and with which they were familiar. It was a survival mode of existence. However, when Jesus calls them, and as simple as that call might have sounded, they are encountered by a reality that is "other," even if they don't have a clue what that "other" is or will look like. It compels them to leave their old way of life for something that is new. As the story unfolds, we realize that they have entered that in between space where they continue to be encountered by Jesus' "otherness." It is a space where they themselves eventually become something "other" than who and what they have been.

This becoming though, does not happen without stepping into unknown, uncertainty, disruption, and disorientation. As much as the disciples have the occasion to get to know who Jesus really is, they are confused and uncertain as to who he is and what his mission is about. We see this in the story of Jesus encounter with Peter when Jesus tells the disciples that he must die. Peter rebukes him, "No, Lord, this won't happen to you," to which Jesus responds, "Get behind me Satan, for you are setting your mind not on

---

11. Matt 4:17, NRSV.

12. Warren Carter places this story in the context of the Roman Empire's control of the fishing industry of which these disciples were a part. Under imperial rule, heavy taxes and other financial burdens were levied against fishermen. In addition, fishermen were considered to be at the lower rungs of the sociopolitical and economic hierarchy. Carter asserts that Jesus' call to follow him "invades and challenges their everyday world controlled by imperial economics. His words make available God's empire/reign and create for those who follow an alternative community and way of life with a different center, values, and structure" (Carter, *Matthew and the Margins*, 120–22).

The Empowering but Unsettling Hope of the Gospel

divine things but on human things."[13] We see it again when James and John approach Jesus asking that they be granted the privilege to sit at his right and left hand when Jesus comes into power. Jesus tells them, "You have no idea what you are asking."[14] Then he confuses them by telling them that greatness will only come by becoming a servant. They don't seem to get it. And of course, they are more than bewildered and confused when Jesus is arrested, unjustly tried, and brutally crucified, so bewildered and confused that they run away leaving Jesus alone. Even after Jesus' resurrection, they have difficulty believing that he has been raised from the dead even after hearing the news from eyewitnesses.[15]

As with us, their pilgrimage of becoming was no where close to an immediate transformation into a blissful world. It was a pilgrimage of living in between what they had been and what they were becoming. It was a pilgrimage full of uncertainty, fear, and doubt, and one in which at times they failed. Yet they stayed in it because somewhere in that pilgrimage they caught a glimpse—an Encuentro and an epiphany!—of God's future, a future they knew to be real and coming towards them, a future which compelled them to keep directing and committing their lives to it, even if they stumbled and fell along the way.

As they finally come to know who Jesus was and what his mission was about, they become faithful leaders of a community, the church. Like the disciples who entered into the uncertain pilgrimage of becoming, so it was with this small but growing community. We might even say that just like the disciples, this community existed in a borderland reality. It was a community that lived on the margins and in the shadows. It was a community that lived in two realms at the same time. It was a heterogeneous community of mixed ethnicities, mixed languages, and mixed cultures. It was a community that stood out as totally "other" from the norms and values of the Roman Empire.

Like the disciples, their growing and maturing faith was a pilgrimage of living in between what they had been and what they were becoming. They discovered gifts and powers they didn't know they had, and along with that power, they came to recognize a courage and resilience they could never have imagined themselves to possess. But make no mistake, this was not a bliss-filled transformation. To be sure, it brought considerable joy as

---

13. Mark 8:30–33, NRSV.
14. Mark 10:35–40, NRSV.
15. Mark 16: 9–12, NRSV.

the New Testament letters testify. But it also brought suffering, angst, grief, uncertainty, and unknowing as they encountered persecution, imprisonment, dehumanization, and death. Yet that is the paradox of the faith. It was in this strange, bewildering, and at times confusing pilgrimage of becoming that they were transformed into a culture of life that resisted the enormous powers of death in which they and so much of the world was situated. It was a culture guided by a vision of God's future, not as a far off distant reality, but as a future that had come near to them in the person of Jesus, the Christ and a future to which their lives were increasingly directed and committed.

Living Into Baptismal Identity— Stepping into Liminal Space

The idea of baptismal life as a stepping into liminal and unknowing space will likely seem strange, perhaps even a bit heretical, since for most Christians it is a sacrament of assurance. Stepping into the waters of baptism, we are given the assurance that we have been united with Jesus the Christ in his death and resurrection. Whatever else befalls or threatens our life, we live with that hope and assurance. Of this, there can be no question. Having said that, however, we must assert that baptism is much more than a one-and-done ritual of assurance, that once it is over we can go on with our settled life as though nothing happened.

It matters not whether baptism was given to us as infants or children, or whether we decided it for ourselves as adults, baptism is a sacrament of becoming, a sacrament of living between what we have been and what we are yet to be; it is a sacrament of leaving what is old for what is new. One might say that it is our entrance into the transformational pilgrimage of becoming a culture of life. And as we have seen, this transformational becoming is always a stepping into a space of "otherness," unknown and uncertainty. Luther said as much in his instruction on baptism. Regardless of how we came into the baptismal life, whether as an infant or as an adult, *baptism brings us into a life of dying and rising with Christ*. And what is dying and rising but leaving what is old for what is new, of living between that which is dying and that which is rising? It is stepping into the liminal space of being in between what we have been and what we are becoming.

Luther spoke of baptism as a gift that is given. Even if we choose it for ourselves, it is still a gift. It is a gift because God is the one doing all the action and work of putting to death what is old and raising up what is new. Like any gift, however, it is not given to be placed on a shelf and put out of sight. It is a gift given to be used daily! The right use of this gift has everything to do with what he called the "slaying of the old creature" and the "raising up of the new," a life of dying and rising. For Luther, the rite of baptism consists of two significant parts. The first is being dipped or immersed into water, and the second is emerging out of the water.[16]

> These two parts, being dipped under the water and emerging from it, point to the power of and effect of baptism, which is nothing else than the slaying of the old creature and the resurrection of the new new creature, both of which must continue in us our whole lives long. Thus a Christian life is nothing else than a daily baptism, begun once and continuing ever after. For we must keep at it without ceasing, always purging whatever pertains to the old creature, so that whatever belongs to the new creature may come forth.[17]

Luther was adamant. *Dying and rising is a daily pilgrimage of living between what we have been and what we are becoming.* It is a pilgrimage that begins in baptism but it is not completed until we die. However, living into this pilgrimage is not simply a matter of passively waiting for its completion. It has everything to do with being acted upon by the Spirit so as to actively recognize and be awakened to how this "old creature" is working in us, how it is affecting our behaviors and relationships with others, and how our lives are impacting the lives of our neighbors, creation, and the world. Living into baptismal dying and rising is not only to be awakened to old and non life giving behaviors, it is to engage in the work of actively resisting those behaviors and purging ourselves of them. Hear what Luther said.

> Now, when we enter Christ's kingdom (baptism is our entrance into God's kingdom), this corruption must daily decrease so that the longer we live the gentler and more patient and meek we become, and the more we break away from greed, hatred, envy, and pride. This is the right use of baptism among Christians, signified by baptizing with water. Where this does not take place but rather

---

16. Luther's comment about immersion should not be interpreted to mean that he thought it was the only means by which baptism should be administered. In an annotated note, Stjerna comments that while immersion was customary in the sixteenth century, the practice of infusion, pouring the baptismal water over the child's head three times began already in the fourteenth century. The practice and means by which baptism is administered does not alter Luther's understanding and what it signifies (*TLC*, 399).

17. *TLC*, 399.

the old creature is given free rein and continually grows stronger, baptism is not being used but resisted.[18]

If the baptismal life is one of stepping into liminal space, then one way to understand what Luther has described as the right use of baptism is through the lens offered by Alanís. Baptismal life is living in the liminal and transitional space where we stand on the threshold of sacred encounters. It is the threshold where we experience Encuentro, encounters that are epiphanies, encounters that awaken us and bring us into new awarenesses about our neighbors and their needs, epiphanies that bring us into new awarenesses of ourselves, who we are in the world, and who we are in relationship to God and our neighbors. They are Encuentro experiences where we are encountered by the "otherness" of the gospel, an "otherness" that opens our consciousness and gives us a new vision of the new being we are becoming. They are Encuentro experiences that call us into a daily resistance and purging of what is old in us. It is a daily resistance and purging that will always bring us into the existential tension of living between what is old and what is new.[19]

The Pilgrimage of Becoming in A Culture of Self-Absorbed Narcissism

Louise Kretzshcmar reminded us of our propensity to privatize the faith, that is, to limit the gospel to our private and personal spiritual concerns without hearing its radical call to be reconciled with all who have been alienated, disenfranchised, and relegated to the margins of life. In our self-absorbed culture of narcissism, that is exactly what we have done with the sacrament of baptism. We have privatized it so that its message of dying, rising, and liberation is restricted to our personal and private salvation. In this privatized view, baptism's powerful word of reconciliation with God is limited only to our personal and private relationship with God, yet, its equally powerful message to be reconciled with our neighbor and the world, especially those on the fringes and margins of life, is largely ignored or blatantly disregarded. The privatization of baptism is what prevents us from recognizing and heeding sacred encounters. Privatizing baptism prevents us from being encountered by the "otherness" of the gospel and the

---

18. *TLC*, 400.
19. Alanís, "Third Spaces, slide 4.

"otherness" of the neighbors, cultures, ethnicities, genders, and languages that are different from our own, all encounters that have the potential to awaken us to the new being into which baptism has called us.

Given what we have just said about using the gift of baptism, our privatization of baptism is equivalent to putting it on a shelf where it is ignored. When tucked away on our private shelves, baptism is not allowed to speak, awaken, or lead us into pilgrimages of transformation and becoming. We might go through the ritual of saying words, yet it is not allowed to do much by way of compelling or empowering us to leave what is old for what is new.

Yet, if baptism is our entrance into the liminal space of dying and rising with Jesus the Christ, then that dying and rising has every bit as much to do with dying to old behaviors and attitudes that contribute to and participate in the dehumanization, exploitation, domination and marginalization of other human beings. In short, it means dying to behaviors and attitudes that prevent our sibling human beings the ability to live in the authentic fulness of their God-given humanity. In our culture of entitlement and privilege, rightly using and living into the gift of our baptismal identity means being encountered so that we are awakened to our active and complicit participation in racism and in the increasing economic divides between rich and poor; it means being awakened to our contributions to global warming and the devastations we are wreaking on the earth and all of its life giving resources. It means being awakened to the extent we deprive others of the basics of life by our indulgent and consumeristic ways of living. The list can go on.

For many, this will seem like a litany intended to take everyone into the Pit of shame and despair, a litany that overwhelms us with what is wrong with us. Yes, to an extent that's what it is. However, in the baptismal pilgrimage of becoming, this intent is not to engender shame. Rather, it is to "call a thing what it is." It is cutting through the pretenses and illusions we have of ourselves to see the extent of our brokenness, not just our personal and private brokenness, but our brokenness and alienation from our human siblings and the earth, and the extent to which we are not living into our full and authentic humanity. Following Luther's instruction on baptism, its intent is to make us aware of our corruption so that we may live in the pilgrimage of daily decreasing it. The purpose of this litany is to awaken us to what needs restraint and decreasing so that is not given free rein to have its way with us.

Part I: The World We Live In

If truth be told, keeping our baptism privatized and neglecting its pilgrimage of becoming is to allow our greed, hatred, envy, and pride, all of the ingredients that contribute to dehumanization, exploitation, domination, and marginalization have their way with us. It does nothing but allow them to grow stronger and wreak their devastations even more. If we begin to think of it this way, we begin to see that the effects and power of our baptism extend way beyond our personal lives and even our personal salvation. Living into the baptismal pilgrimage of our baptism is an unsettling and disquieting venture into unknowing, uncertainty, and disorientation. Yet paradoxically, it is a pilgrimage that leads us out of our self-absorbed and narcissistic ways of living into a transformation that empowers both us and those whose lives we touch to live more fully into our authentic humanity and human vocations.

I conclude this section and chapter by returning to the story of the encounter between Allison and me. While it is a story of reconciliation, healing, and the beginning of new ways of relating, one cannot underestimate the disquieting disruption that came for both of us as we encountered the truth that old and settled ways of being were not helpful or life giving, that they were in fact destructive. I reiterate the point: this unsettling encounter awakened both of us to truths that we had long kept at a distance or outright denied. In my case, I did not learn *about* racism and white supremacy; I came to *know* it as it existed in me and how it was being manifested in my behaviors towards Allison. For her part, Allison discovered a power in her life story that, heretofore, she had never recognized. To use Alanís' language, we were both encountered by each other's "otherness," an "otherness" though which a holy Spirit awakened us to new possibilities and new vocational directions. For both of us, it was—and still is—the gospel's empowering but unsettling hope!

A Transitional Word

With this chapter, we come to the end of Part I of this discussion, "The World We Live In—Between Death and Life." We now turn our attention to Part II, "Becoming What We Are Yet To Be." The core of Part II will be a close look at Luther's instruction as it is explicated in his *Large Catechism*. The goal of this exploration is not to restate Luther's explanations to the catechism's chief parts. Rather it is to probe them and allow them to ask us questions that might open the window to a new understanding of what it means to leave survival modes of existence for baptismal vocation in the midst of our present perils and threats.

As we turn our attention to the *Large Catechism* and the relevance of its instruction for living into the baptismal pilgrimage of becoming, I am reminded of something Brueggemann said in his book, *Finally Comes the Poet:*

> The gospel is too readily heard and taken for granted, as though it contained no unsettling news and no unwelcome threat. What began as news in the gospel is easily assumed, slotted, and conveniently dismissed. We depart having heard, but without noticing the urge to transformation that is not readily compatible with our comfortable believing that asks little and receives less. The gospel is thus a truth widely held, but a truth greatly reduced. It is a truth that has been flattened, trivialized, and rendered inane. Partly, the gospel is simply an old habit among us, neither valued nor questioned.[20]

I suggest that what Brueggemann says of the current state of how the gospel is preached and heard in most congregations is an accurate description of how Luther's catechetical instruction has been used and heard: it has been slotted and reduced to a required document that children and adolescents must learn in order to become members of a Lutheran congregation. Once the catechumen is graduated, the catechism is taken for granted and mostly rendered irrelevant if not inane. Consistent with Brueggemann's comment that we do not notice the gospel's "urge to transformation," Luther's instruction holds little to no value for most adults in transforming their faith or empowering them to live into their baptismal pilgrimages, especially in our present moment of peril and threat.

What is needed is a different way of hearing Luther's instruction, a way that is different from our one dimensional understanding of its purpose in our personal and congregational lives. I do not propose that we approach Luther's instruction in the same old familiar patterns of adult study, patterns that tend to help us think about the faith and maintain it as an old habit, yet do precious little to challenge and lead us into our baptismal pilgrimages. Rather, I suggest we approach it in the manner that Brueggemann suggests when he says,

> To address the issue of a truth greatly reduced requires us to be *poets that speak against a prose world*. By prose I refer to a world that is organized in settled formulae, so that even pastoral prayers and

---

20. Brueggemann, *Finally Comes the Poet*, 1–2.

love letters sound like memos. By poetry, I do not mean rhyme, rhythm, or meter, but language that moves like Bob Gibson's fast ball, that jumps at the right moment, that breaks open old worlds with surprise, abrasion, and pace.[21]

He goes on. "It is rather the ready, steady surprising proposal that the real world in which God invites us to live is not the one made available by the rulers of this age."[22] I suggest that this was precisely Luther's intent when he imparted his instruction to the church: "to open up old worlds with surprise, abrasion and pace," and to offer a world where our "existence is shaped by the news of the gospel." In a difficult and perilous time such as we presently live, the opportunity to hear this powerful voice is missed when we leave Luther's instruction in its settled patterns and formulae within our personal, church and congregational lives, when we adapt and conform his instruction to what we want to hear rather than allowing our lives to be awakened by what it is actually saying to us. Even if his instruction does not have the poetic character to which Brueggemann refers,[23] it is nevertheless a prophetic voice, and one which we need to hear in these difficult times. Only then can we hear its visions of new existence and possibilities with surprise and urgency.

It might seem strange to think of Luther's instruction as having a prophetic voice. Prophetic speech is associated with judgment, and angry judgment at that! If truth be told, there are times Luther's instruction sounds exactly like that, angry judgement. If one is not careful, it can sound like law, punishment and even rejection. It will sound like the work and speech that came from the prophets who were in fact bringing a harsh word of judgment to Israel and Judah for their failures in living as people in covenant with God.

Pastoral work and speech, on the other hand, are associated with comfort, hope, encouragement, forgiveness, grace, and unconditional acceptance! We associate it with images of the Good Shepherd, the One who attends the flock and goes after the lost. The pastoral voice through which we hear Luther's instruction is the voice embedded in the familiar Reformation theme, *justification by grace through faith*, the voice that declares we are saved by God's grace alone and not by our own merits. Without question the pastoral voice always brings a comforting and hopeful word—and

---

21. Brueggemann, *Finally Comes the Poet*, 3.
22. Brueggemann, *Finally Comes the Poet*, 3.
23. Brueggemann, *Finally Coms the Poet*, 4.

that is as it should be! *But if that's the catechism's only voice to which we tune our ears, we significantly reduce its volume and its capacity to lead us into baptism's pilgrimage of becoming.* Let me be clear. The fact that I am calling attention to the prophetic voice in Luther's instruction does not in any way take away from the centrality of justification by grace through faith in Luther's instruction. As a matter of fact, I suggest that Luther's prophetic voice is in truth a profound word of grace and unmerited love!

Prophetic speech and pastoral speech are never as separate or distinguishable as we have made them! They are two sides of the same coin, two aspects of the same work and speech. Pastoral work and speech, when done honestly and correctly, are always prophetic; prophetic work and speech, when done honestly and correctly, are always pastoral! What makes both of these actions one and the same is that they are always the work of bringing people into right relationship with God! While the prophets' harshest words of judgment and punishment directed to Judah and Israel spoke of the approaching destruction God was about to inflict on them, there was always behind those words the conviction that this action was but the beginning of God's creation of something new, the beginning of God calling his people back into right relationship with her, a calling to return to the vocation into which she had called them in the first place.

Words of judgment and punishment are never spoken without an explicit or implicit hope in God's faithfulness to God's life-giving creativity and to the covenant she made. The fact of the matter is that Luther's instruction is full of words of judgment, full of words that call God's people to accountability, full of words that indict people for their negligence and taking God for granted. At the same time, his instruction is clearly full of the hope of God's faithfulness, full of the vision of new life, existence and possibilities as God's redeemed, forgiven, and reconciled people! Only when we hear both the prophetic and pastoral voice of Luther's instruction will it become for us a living and vibrant proclamation that awakens our faith into an imaginative and enlivened faith rather than a mere instruction on what to believe and how to adhere to a flattened doctrinal instruction. Only when we hear the prophetic and pastoral voices that are in the *Large Catechism* will we hear its awakening and empowering voice that holds the potential to lead us into our authentic human vocation of becoming, the vocation of becoming and living into a culture of life that resists the powers of death.

Part II

Becoming What We Are Yet to Be

4

What God, Lord, or Power Defines Your World?

Questions—Not Answers

WHEN THE OLD TESTAMENT prophets spoke their words, sometimes harsh words of judgment, punishment, or impending doom, their intent was to awaken God's people to the extent they had taken God for granted and the extent to which they had dangerously gone awry and off track from the covenental relationship she had established with them. We know their reactions to the prophets' words. They refused to hear or allow those prophetic words into their hearts so as to open themselves to a close examination of how their lives and life styles were a total contradiction to that covenantal relationship. They refused to allow the prophetic words to question their life. In refusing such a questioning, they chose to take God for granted thinking that they had God well in hand, rather than allow God's prophetic words to intervene and restore them to a right relationship. Hearing prophetic voices means opening our hearts to the questions those voices pose for our life and existence. And often they are questions that disquiet and disrupt us, yet they are life giving voices. Prophetic voices are often the voices of a sacred encounter, an Encuentro, even if that encounter will not feel sacred.

If we are to hear Luther's prophetic voice in the *Large Catechism*, then we need to open ourselves to the questions that instructional and prophetic

Part II: Becoming What We Are Yet to Be

voice poses rather than hear his instruction as a way of having God matters settled, well in hand, and under control. This may seem strange and contradictory since Luther's language and pedagogical style is to give clear answers that leave the impression if one has these answers, then one has God matters packaged and well under control. But as Kirsi Stjerna says, "The pedagogical format and easy flow of the language Luther employs in the Large Catechism should not fool the reader to dismiss its theological ammunition."[1] From my perspective, that ammunition has everything to do with the deep, incisive questions Luther puts in front of the reader when he applies the meaning of a particular commandment, article of the creed, or a petition of the Lord's Prayer to the worldly realities of greed, hate, pride, and prejudice. If we hear these questions and allow them to question our life and the things we take for granted, then Luther's instruction holds the potential to encounter and awaken us with abrasive surprise, disquieting alarm, yet the powerful hope of becoming and living into a culture of life!

In his book, *Living Faith*, Jacques Ellul, the French philosopher and lay theologian, speaks to faith's illuminating power when it poses questions rather than provides settled answers. In this regard, he makes a clear distinction between faith and religious belief, a distinction, in my opinion, that helps us approach Luther's instruction with new ears. Simply put, Ellul said that faith poses questions while religious belief answers them.[2] Similar to Brueggemann, Ellul noted that faith always addresses the believer with the prospect that the way things are is not necessarily the way they must be or should be; therefore, faith always calls our settled ways of seeing and managing life into question, including the settled ways we assume or imagine who we are as human beings and what we think are our purposes in life. Faith assumes nothing, and it takes nothing for granted, especially God. Like Brueggemann, Ellul's notion that faith always asks questions means that life can never be reduced to a settled formulaic pattern, for it is always changing. More importantly, faith can never be reduced to settled formulae or easy answers, for faith itself is always changing. While the substance of faith does not change, its relevance, meaning, how we understand it in our present circumstances, and what it is calling and leading us into is always changing.

When faith responds to our questions with more questions, it is encountering us and leading us into a life of becoming—that place of standing between what we have been and what we are yet to be. When religious

---

1. *TLC*, 285.
2. Ellul, *Living Faith*, 99.

beliefs give answers and certainty but asks no questions, the transformational work of becoming what we are yet to be will not happen.

To put it another way, the questions with which faith confronts us lead us into the disorienting place of unknowing and uncertainty. That's what questions always do, at least if we listen to them and allow them to do their work with us. If and when we allow ourselves the grace to sit with those questions and allow them to stir things up, they paradoxically will hold the potential to encounter us and lead us into an awakening of renewed faith and vocation. If we approach Luther's instruction with an openness and willingness to hear and have these questions posed to us, then it might well be that his instruction will impact and awaken us the way Brueggemann described: it will come at us like Bob Gibson's fastball, jumping at the right moment to break open our old worlds with surprise, abrasion, and pace.

The Real World of Faith

Like most preachers, whenever I have preached on a topic like love your neighbor or forgive your enemies, it is not uncommon to hear the comment, "That's well and good, pastor, but that's not the real world we live in." Sometimes the person uttering that response will go a step further and try to teach me what the world is really like. "In the real world you have to protect yourself." "In the real world, you can't go around loving everybody or you'll get taken advantage of." "In the real world, forgiveness doesn't work." "In the real world, you have to work hard for what you want or you'll never amount to much." On one occasion, I actually overheard someone make this comment, referring to me, "Well, when he grows up he'll find out what the world is really like and how it works." Even if it was intended as humor, it spoke to a truth: what is real to the eyes of faith is not real to the eyes of the world. To paraphrase Paul, what is real to the eyes of faith will appear to the world as unreal, foolish, unwise, fanciful, and even immature.[3]

Following the idea that Luther's instruction in the *Large Catechism* poses as many questions as it provides answers, its most fundamental question, particularly in this age of peril and threat, is this: Who are the gods, lords, and powers to which you turn to define what is real in your world? To most Christians the response to that question may seem obvious. Yet when the *Large Catechism* begins to drill down, that question may be more revealing than we might have thought. This is especially so in a culture of

3. 1 Cor 1:20–25, NRSV.

self-absorbed narcissism where our proclivity is to conform the gospel to our way of seeing and being in the world rather than to have our world conform to the reality of the gospel.

In what follows, we look at four ways that Luther's explications of the first commandment and the first two articles of the creed set forth what constitutes reality in the real world of faith: trust versus control, standing in unknowing and uncertainty, trusting the interdependency of creation, and power turned upside down.

Trust vs. Control

I share a story. One Sunday, not long after the horrors of 9/11, I was talking with a gentleman after church about the events that had happened. In the course of the conversation I commented that one of the possible good things to come out of it all was the recognition that we Americans are as vulnerable to the powers of evil as the rest of the world, that we might now know what it's like to live with the reality of fear and vulnerability the rest of the world lives with on a daily basis. I went on to say that it might offer us an opportunity to be in solidarity with those who suffer this kind of vulnerability and devastation on a daily basis. He quickly retorted with intensity, "No! We are entitled to all the security we can get because we can afford it!" He made no reference to being able to understand the rest of the world, much less increasing our solidarity with the sufferings of our neighbors. What mattered to him was the security to which he felt we were entitled because we could afford it. In reality, his intense reaction was a manifestation of his unregulated fear, a fear precipitated by the reality that we are not always able to control things that threaten our way of life. We were vulnerable, just as we are now. Yet, in his conventional way of thinking, our perceived ability to afford and control things meant that we were—and are—entitled to live with immunity to vulnerability. In the horrors of 9/11, that immunity was punctured and penetrated!

What this gentleman unwittingly revealed in both his words and his attitude was that the god and power defining his real world was the god of wealth, privilege, and entitlement. These were the things to which he looked for refuge, security and well being and to which he appealed to preserve his way of life. This in spite of the fact that this conversation took place immediately after Christian worship in which we confessed our ultimate faith and trust in the God the creator of heaven and earth.

What God, Lord, or Power Defines Your World?

In Luther's instruction, it is significant that he begins by setting forth the bed rock foundation for the Christian faith's perspective of what constitutes the real world and the reality in which the Christian is situated. The real world of faith is a world of trust wherein God gives the clear directive not to let unregulated fear take charge of our life, but trust that she will give life, especially in times of trouble and danger. That command is based on one fundamental premise: God is the creator of all creation and is to be trusted for all good, well being, refuge and security. This foundational conviction and orientation is asserted in God's directive in the first commandment, you shall have no God other than me, and then again in our confessional statement in the first article of the creed, I believe in God the creator of everything that exists. It is further stated in God's directive in the second commandment that we are to call upon God's Name in all times of trouble, difficulty, or threat, with the assurance that such a call will be heard and responded to.

On the one hand, the idea of God being the creator of everything who is to be trusted for all of life will sound like a "no-brainer." What Christian doesn't say that? On the other hand, when it becomes a question, it is no longer a no-brainer statement to be taken for granted. Rather, it is a question that poignantly asks whether our life is being governed by unregulated fear and control, or by trust in God's goodness. In Luther's language, it is asking us where we are placing our heart when our lives are under threat or danger of any kind, to what are we attaching our heart for all goodness and well being. Moreover, when these foundational statements and beliefs turn into questions, they are asking us: to whom or what are we turning to define what is real in our life? In whose words or in what powers are we placing our trust to define what constitutes the real world? In whose words or in what powers are we placing our trust when we are faced with the fears and anxieties that come when we must venture into places of unknowing and uncertainty?

In a moving exposition on Psalm 77 in which he observes the Psalm's speaker moving from self-centered faith to an awareness of the God who does not conform to his expectations, Walter Brueggemann commented on a central characteristic of narcissism and a narcissistic culture: "One of the important ingredients in such immobilizing narcissism is the flattening of imagination so that the person is incapable of thinking of life other than it is, or incapable of thinking of life beyond self.[4] In other words, self-ab-

---

4. Brueggemann, *Virus as a Summons to Faith*, 48.

sorbed narcissism prevents us from trusting in God's life-giving goodness in such a way that we are able to imagine a life beyond what we know and are trying to hold on to.

What Brueggemann observed of our culture's narcissism is exactly what Luther observed already in the sixteenth century and noted in his explanation to the first commandment.

> There are some who think they have God and everything they need when they have money and property; they trust in them and boast in them so stubbornly and securely that they care for no one else. They, too, have a god—mammon by name, that is money and property—on which they set their whole heart. This is the most common idol on earth.[5]

When people think they have everything they need in their wealth, property, status or power, and when they are consumed by what they have or must pursue so that they care about no one else other than themselves, their world and lives have become defined by what they have or the possessions they are pursuing. They are preoccupied with self. They are then no longer able to see or imagine life beyond themselves and what they have. What Luther said about individuals applies to communities, institutions, organizations, and even congregations. Anytime we are consumed by what we have or must hold on to, our lives become defined by those very things and objects. Luther's words align precisely with Brueggemann's point that when our privilege, entitlement and possessions define us, we lose our capacity and ability to imagine any kind of life beyond our selves, what we know, what we are pursuing, or what we want to hold on to. In the brief illustration above, this is exactly the dynamic that drove the gentleman's reactivity. He was unable to allow his faith to envision anything beyond the secure life to which he felt entitled; nor could he allow his faith to give him the courage to enter into the vulnerable place of uncertainty and unknowing that called him to let go of his control.

Standing in Unknowing and Uncertainty

If the truth be told and in the face of all the chaos and perils that presently threaten us, we are in a place of disorienting unknown and uncertainty, a place that is repugnant to a culture for whom certainty and control are

5. *TLC*, 301.

fundamental values of its "real world." It is not clear that we can have what we want when we want it; it is not clear that we can hold on to life as we might have had or want it. Despite all of the positive assurances the powers that be want to give us, the future is unknown and uncertain. It is not surprising and certainly understandable that we cry out, "God return us to what we have known!" However, the hard truth is that life as we have known it—whether in our personal, communal, congregational, or even our national life—may never return to what we have known. Which also means that our understanding of who we are as privileged and entitled people may not be the same again either. Let's be honest, it is understandably a place of profound grief and sadness. Letting go of what we have known for a new and unknown future is worthy of grief. But grief is the only way we can begin moving into the unknown of what is new. In this place of disorientation, unknowing, uncertainty, and grief, we are being led to imagine our life and who we are beyond ourselves and what we have known. In this unsettled place, we are driven back to the bedrock foundation of our Christian faith that calls us to trust in this God who is all good and is the source of our refuge, security and well being, especially in times of disruption, threat, and peril.

In this uncertain place, the question is not whether we will have faith. The question is, will it be a faith that allows us to stand in the places of unknowing and vulnerability, in the places of standing between death and life with trust and confidence that God's life giving creativity will give us direction. Or, like the gentleman in the story, will it be a "faith of those without faith" that gives unregulated fear charge of our life to determine the directions and courses of actions we should take in the face of death's powers and devastations? Will it be a trust in God that opens our imaginations and invites us to step into visions beyond the settled lives we have known? Or will it be a faith that keeps us stuck in what has been?

Part of this imagination might be to reimagine our present circumstances and crises. What if our present crises are not just adversities to get through so that we can return to normal, but circumstances and life events that are inviting and challenging us to confront our self-centered and self-absorbed ways of life, or perhaps even challenging us into a new and different kind of obedience and discipleship? To be sure, this kind of imagination is risky at best, and it requires a certain grief in letting go of what has been so that we can embrace what is new. It is the same risky turn that Brueggemann sees in Psalm 77 when the Psalmist cried out, "My grief is this, that God has lost God's power." At the conclusion of his exposition, Brueggemann writes:

> If one is linked to a flat one-dimensional faith, then this verse (the Psalmists grief over God's power) is *a bitter loss of faith*. But if we think in terms of obedience on its way to risky imagination, then this verse is *an opening for new faith* beyond the conventions and routines that secure but do not reckon with God's *awefulness* (God's shocking interventions into our life). This verse stands at a very risky and dangerous place where evangelical faith often stands. And indeed must stand. And as we stand there, we never know in advance if we face *loss of faith* or *opening for new faith*.[6]

I suggest that this is precisely the in-between place in which we are presently standing; it is the place where we are being invited—if not challenged—into new ways of believing, trusting, and obeying. It is a place of being awakened to new and more life giving ways of living and being in the vocations to which our faith is calling us. In spite of how it might seem to us, the trust of which Luther speaks in the first commandment and first article of the creed is a trust that does not expect God to return things to normal or to preserve old settled ways of life. As Brueggemann suggests, it is a trust that relies on God to see us through what is unknown to what is yet to be. It is a trust that allows us to step into a *new faith* that is beyond what has been familiar, flat and unimaginative. It is a trust that finds one's true self—whether that self is an individual, a community, or a congregation—in God's holy and faithful goodness, not in one's self.

For Luther, trust in God for all refuge, security and well being is to imagine one's self beyond one's self-contained world, self-interests, and even beyond one's self-preserving desires. It is to open one's self to an imagination that is stimulated by the Spirit of the gospel to leave the safety and security of what is familiar to venture out into community and solidarity with the neighbor in need, the neighbor who is marginalized, the neighbor who is poor, the neighbor who is a victim of racial injustice and hatred. It is an imagination that invites us to venture from our safety to take risks on behalf of our neighbor, particularly those who are facing harm of any kind. The faith and trust which God directs us to have is not a safe trust as we like to think of it. It is not a trust that leads us to hunker down and protect only ourselves and those around us. Quite the opposite. In times of peril, it is a faith and trust that calls and invites us out of our bunkers to be in the

---

6. Brueggemann, *Virus as a Summons to Faith*, 50.

world for the sake of our neighbor. It is a faith and trust that invites us to abandon our self-centeredness and self-absorption and place ourselves in God's goodness and holiness! It is the faith to which Jesus attested when he said, "The one who loses life saves it; the one who saves life loses it." In Luther's instruction, the first commandment and the first article of the creed awaken us to the reality of a faith that is distinct from the reality of the world: to trust God above everything else is the beginning of the end of self-absorbed and narcissistic control. One might even say that to trust God for all refuge, security, and well being is to enter into a borderland reality.

Trusting the Interdependency of Life

Every Sunday morning when Christian communities of faith gather for worship, a major component of their worship gathering will be their confession of faith expressed in the words of the Apostle's Creed, "I believe in God the creator of all that exists . . ." Generally those words are spoken and confessed without much thought given, if any, to what we are saying about creation and our relationship to the created order. For in saying and confessing those words, we are actually laying claim to a belief that human beings are not masters of the created order, nor is it for them to do with it as they please. As a matter of fact it is quite the reverse. To confess that I believe in God the creator of all things is to say out loud that we believe the real world into which we have been created, restored and called to live is an *interdependent world*. When we declare that God is the creator of everything, we are declaring that God has created an interdependency within the very nature of life and all creation. Nothing, nothing at all, is able to exist on its own or isolated from every other created being, plant, animal or the earth itself. Everything is dependent on everything else in order for the sustenance of life to be maintained. Human beings were not created to control creation or any part of it to serve their self-interests or their self-serving purposes.

Thus when we confess a belief in this God who has created everything, we are in those very words saying that we believe ourselves to live in this interdependency; we are confessing that we have no right whatsoever to exploit others or the earth itself for the sake of our self-indulgent pleasures. We believe God to have created everything so that everyone and everything in the created order will be blessed with life! No exceptions! Hear Luther's words:

> ... God makes all creation help provide the benefits and necessities of life—sun, moon, and stars in the heavens; day and night; air, fire, water, the earth, and all that it yields and brings forth; birds, fish, animals, grain, and all sorts of produce. Moreover, God gives all physical and temporal blessings—good government, peace, security. Thus we learn from this article that none of us has life—or anything else that has been mentioned here or can be mentioned—from ourselves, nor can we by ourselves preserve any of them, however small and unimportant. All this is comprehended in the word "Creator."[7]

It does not take long to realize that in making this statement of faith, the very assumptions of what is real and true in the conventional wisdom of the world, that human beings were created to dominate and use the earth for its own purposes, are seriously and radically questioned.

Jürgen Moltmann speaks to this interdependency when he says that we are in "need of a new understanding of nature and a new picture of the human being—and that means a new experience of God."[8] Why turn to God and theology? Because, in Moltmann's view, it is modern Christian theology that has given rise to the concept of "lordship over the world which was to be exercised by the godlike human being," a lordship that meant all non-human dwellers on the earth, and even the earth itself, "had to be 'subdued' and 'subjected.'"[9] The new experience of God or a new theology of creation, in Moltmann's view, begins with a "new ecological" way of reading the creation narratives. In this regard, he reminds us that in the first creation story,

> the human being is the last being God creates and therefore the most dependent of all God's creations. For their life on earth, human beings are dependent on the existence of animals and plants, air and water, light, daytime and night time, sun, moon, and stars, and without these things they cannot live. Human beings exist only because all other creatures exist ... Whatever their special position and their special tasks may be, human beings are one created being in the great "community of life," and part of nature.[10]

---

7. *TLC*, 354.
8. Moltmann, *Spirit of Hope*, 15.
9. Moltmann, *Spirit of Hope*, 15.
10. Moltmann, *Spirit of Hope*, 18.

What God, Lord, or Power Defines Your World?

Moltmann also reminds us that within the biblical tradition, human beings were not the only creatures who came from dust and into whom the breath of life was breathed. All created beings come from dust, and into all created beings is breathed the holy breath of life. Speaking of creatures other than human beings, Psalm 104 declares and affirms:

> When thou hidest thy face, they are dismayed;
> When thou takest away their breath, they die and return to their dust;
> When thou sendest forth thy Spirit, the are created;
> and thou renewest the face of the ground.[11]

Moltmann's concluding words help us understand the relevance of this view of creation to what we say and confess in the creed.

> It is only when we become aware of our dependence on the life of the earth and the existence of other living things that we shall turn from being what Luther called "proud and unhappy gods" into truly human beings. True knowledge is not power; true knowledge is wisdom.[12]

Our confession that God is the creator of all that exists is not just a statement about who God is. It is a statement that defines what we believe is true and real for the world we inhabit: we human beings are not the center of the world or creation, nor have we been given privileged entitlement to control, subdue and subject it to our whims, desires, and wants. We are co-inhabitants along with every other living thing that inhabits the earth, and are therefore to treat our co-habitants with respect and humility; for God dwells in them as much as God dwells in us. Needless to say, what we confess to believe about what is true and real for the world radically questions all of the assumed and settled beliefs that the conventional wisdom of a self-indulged world has taught us to accept. The conventional thinking of the world, including much of its popular religious thinking, teaches us that the creation and environment are there for us to control in the pursuit of our self-interests and pleasures; we are able to use it and do what we want with it because we can afford it. In direct contrast, the faith in God that we confess every time we confess the words of the Apostle's Creed is about trusting the way of interdependence rather than the way of self-preserving control that serves self-absorbed interests and cares nothing for what that control does to neighbor, the earth, its resources, or the environment.

11. Ps 104: 29–30, NRSV.
12. Moltmann, *Spirit of Hope*, 20.

Part II: Becoming What We Are Yet to Be

The first commandment and the first article of the creed awaken us to the Christian faith's definition of what is true and real for the world. It is placing our trust and confidence, not just in the fact that God's life giving and sustaining creativity will provide life, but trusting in how God has created and ordered the world so that all of creation can have life. It is trusting that such life giving and sustaining creativity is manifested in the interdependency of all creation, and trusting, therefore, that our vocation is to live interdependently with all of creation rather than control or master it for our self-interests.

Power Turned Upside Down

We live, move and have our being in a world of many gods and lords! The gods and lords of this world ask, require, tempt and seduce us into placing our trust in them with the promise that in return for our servitude they will give us power, power to have what we want, power to overcome any adversity in life, power to have and live the good life. In short, they promise to empower us to control and win at the game of life.

These gods and lords are everywhere. They are in the workplace, in the market square and mall, on the internet, in our politics and political ideologies, and even in our churches. They are the gods and lords that tell us how to achieve success, how to climb the corporate ladder, how to dress for power, how to associate with the right people, how to accumulate wealth, how to find romance and intimacy, and how to find pleasure in life. They are the gods and lords of the American Dream that tell us we are our own gods and are entitled to have anything we want and can afford. They tell us there are no limits or boundaries to what we can have in life. They are also the gods and lords of privilege, power, and domination who seduce us into believing that all persons are not created equal, that certain classes and races of people are more privileged than others.

Indeed, we are surrounded by hordes of gods and lords, all proffering "salvation" of one kind or another. They are the religious gods and lords whose goal is to entertain us in "worship" that resembles an emotionally charged and entertaining stage production. They are like the false prophets of the Old Testament, deceiving us with false messages of security, wealth and success; they are prophets who refuse to "call a thing what it is."

In the midst of this mass of gods and lords that ask for our servitude and "worship," the Christian community gathers, and along with our confession that we believe in God the creator of all things, we confess that we "believe in Jesus Christ, God's only Son our Lord . . ." Just like the creed's first article, this second article puts forth a religious belief that on the surface is a "no-brainer." What Christian doesn't believe these words? But just like the first article, it is a "no-brainer" until it becomes a question. While it is easy to mouth and say these words, what is not so easy to recognize is that in making this confession, we are actually making a statement that in the real world as defined by our faith, we entrust ourselves to a power that contradicts every notion of power proffered by the gods and lords of this world. And that is where it becomes a question. For at the very same time we say and confess these words, they ask us, "In this world of many lords and gods, who do you say that Jesus is? To what sort of lord and power are you entrusting your life?"

In a world of entitled privilege, power is found in wealth, in being able to afford what one wants when one wants it. It is found in the illusory belief that we can be immune from vulnerability to danger, threat, or suffering if we are strong enough and maintain control over whatever it is that we perceive to be a threat to our life. It is found by defeating anything or anyone that stands in the way of our self-interests and self-pursuits. It is found by subjugating and dehumanizing those we perceive as threats to our way of life, persons like unwanted immigrants, persons that have different religious beliefs, persons whose skin color is different, or persons who have an ethnicity and culture other than our own. In a world of privileged entitlement, power is found in manipulating, coercing, and controlling others to see life, the world, and even God, through the same lens as ours. In the reality of the world, having control means being able to escape into an illusory world believing that such an escape will offer freedom from vulnerability and pain; it means ridding the world of perceived threats to a way of life. That's why the messages of the lords and gods of this world are seductive and marketable—they sell!

In the midst of the messages of the lords and gods of this world, especially when they are cloaked in religious and even Christian rhetoric, the question Jesus posed to Peter becomes all the more relevant: "Who do you say that I am?" Even more important is our response to that question. When Jesus says that because of who he is and what he teaches, he will suffer and die, Peter finds that prediction repugnant and rebels—to which Jesus responds, "Get behind me Satan. You are setting your mind not on divine things, but on human things?"[13] In effect, Jesus was telling Peter that he grossly misunderstands who Jesus is and the nature of his power. What if Jesus were to ask us that question, and we were to respond with the same sort of denial as Peter did, "Oh surely that won't happen to you". And what if Jesus were to respond to us the same way as he did to Peter, "Get behind me Satan! You don't get who I really am or what my mission is." I suspect we would be more than offended. But in effect, Jesus would be asking the same thing of us that he asked Peter: What sort of power are you looking for in Jesus? How do you expect Jesus' power to make itself known? Is it a power to which you are willing to give yourself?

Although Luther makes no particular or direct reference to a theology of the cross in his explication of the second article, its presence is evident and unmistakable in the unequivocal distinction he makes between the power of Jesus the Christ and the power of the lords of this world. Jesus' power is a power unlike the power of this world, and moreover, it is not a power easily recognized as power by this world—if recognized at all. His power is not established through wealth, "not with silver and gold."[14] Neither is it established through the domination and destruction of his enemies and those who opposed him. In fact, he suffers and dies at their hands! In the popular parlance of our day, Jesus allows himself to be "a loser!" Moreover, Jesus' power does not come from lofty family lineage. His mother is a lowly, young, unmarried woman, and his adopted father is a carpenter, not exactly positions of status or power in the Empire's hierarchical social structures. This is not a lineage that catapults one into positions of power. There is nothing about Jesus' person or lineage that commends him to be a person of power. Nothing at all.

Yet, that is precisely the point! To the conventional wisdom of the world and its criteria for determining lordship and power, Jesus looks to be nothing more than a powerless and helpless human being, a human being who does not try to control or coerce the world around him, a human being who is as subjected to the powers of death as those to whom he preached and proclaimed good news. Yet it is in this "powerless and helpless human being" that God's power intervenes into the world to offer a new and alternative way of having life and power in the face of death, hidden though it may be! When one drills down and discovers the extent to which our confession of faith explicates a sharp contrast between Jesus' power and the

---

13. Mark 8: 31–33 NRSV.
14. *TLC*, 357.

power of worldly lords, we are all of a sudden confronted with the realization that to make such a confession means we are following a leader who is leading us into a kind of life and power that is radically different from what the lords and gods of the world proffer as salvation. It is a way that can at times make us appear foolish, unwise, naive, and even immature.

We do not follow a conquering hero as some want to purport. We do not follow someone who wanted to create a white nationalistic religion of power. We believe that to claim Jesus as Lord means we follow the way of humility instead of domination; to have Jesus as Lord means we follow the way of equity and respect for every human being instead of dehumanization and domination; to follow Jesus means that we have solidarity and community with those who suffer, those who have been marginalized and disenfranchised. It means following the way of the cross as a way to life, even when that cross leads us into death.

Look closely at the passion narrative. When Jesus' adversaries come to arrest him in the garden, Peter immediately goes into survival mode, pulling out his sword to start a fight, He even cuts off the ear of Malchus, a servant of the high priest.[15] And what does Jesus do? He tells him to put the sword away, and in effect gives himself over to the power of those who came to take him away. No resistance. When he is put on trial, he offers no powerful or masterful defense other than to tell the truth of who he is and what he preached, a truth telling that brought scorn and torment. When brought before Pilate, he knows full well what is about to happen. He suffers the torment and abuse of the Roman soldiers, all without an attempt to resist or run. He goes to the cross, bearing its humiliating and overwhelming pain, yet he does not ask God for revenge. Rather he asks God to forgive his unjust killers because they don't know what they are doing. There is but one point to this whole story: the way of the cross will, in the eyes of the world, always lead to apparent defeat. Yet our confession that Jesus is Lord means that we believe the powers of the world have been turned upside down, even when it appears they have won the day. Ask Dietrich Bonhoeffer.

Luther's words at the end of his instruction on this article summarize it well: "Indeed, the entire Gospel that we preach depends on the proper understanding of this article."[16] This "right understanding" is not about having the right words or formulae to define who Jesus is. It is the "right understanding" that comes from living in defeat when the powers of death have

15. John 18:10, NRSV.
16. *TLC*, 358.

had their way with us, when we are unable to win at the game of life, or when we have put ourselves on the line for justice and truth, but find ourselves coming up short, yet at the very same time trusting with our heart that those powers do not have the final word about our life or the life of the world. We turn again to the words of James Cone that speak directly to this hope.

> That God could "make a way out of no way" in Jesus' cross was truly absurd to the intellect, yet profoundly real in the souls of black folk. Enslaved blacks who first heard the Gospel message seized on the power of the cross. Christ crucified manifested God's loving and liberating presence in the contradictions of black life—that transcendent presence in the lives of black Christians that empowered them to believe that ultimately, in God's eschatological future, they would not be defeated by the "troubles of this world," no matter how great and painful their suffering. Believing this paradox, this absurd claim of faith, was only possible through God's "amazing grace" and the gift of faith, grounded in humility and repentance. There was no place for the proud and the mighty, for people who think that God called them to rule over others. The cross was God's critique of power—white power—with powerless love, snatching victory out of defeat.[17]

The power of the cross is exactly what Cone described. It is God's critique of power, white power in the context to which he was writing, but a critique of any power that seeks to exercise domination, dehumanization, exploitation, or otherwise attempts to have control over others. It is powerless love that snatches victory out of defeat, a strange victory on which faith bases its hope.

The point of this discussion is that as Christians we are called to be in the world, yet live in it with a very different perspective of what is real, even as we live amid death's perils and threats. We have been called to leave a life controlled by unregulated fear, self-preservation and self-protecting control for a life of trust in the life giving and sustaining creativity of God. But such a trust is not passive. It is not a trust that sits back and lets the powers and ways of dehumanizing hate, exploiting greed, or dominating power have their demonic ways with us or with our neighbor. It is a trust that calls us into an active life of obedience to the directives God has set forth about what it means to be human, and what it means for human beings to be in relationship with each other and treat each other as human beings. To use Moltmann's language, it is a trust that leads and compels us

17. Cone, *Cross and The Lynching Tree*, 2

to resist the powers and devastations of any power that seeks to undo life, even as the dangers are growing. For Luther, translating our trust in God's life giving creativity into an active resistance against the powers of death that threaten to undo life is the very vocational life and pilgrimage to which the Christian has been called. It is a life lived under the cross, a vocational life summed up in Jesus' words, "You shall love your neighbor as yourself." In his instruction on the last seven commandments Luther sets forth what this vocational life under the cross looks like in the ordinary affairs of family, human relations, marriage, and business. And to that discussion we now turn.

5

Living into Vocation
Life under the Cross

Trust, Obedience, and Mindfulness

WE HAVE NOTED THROUGHOUT this discussion that in our self-absorbed culture, matters having to do with God and faith have been privatized. When faith is privatized, we don't care much for things like accountability, responsibility to others, or allowing faith to question or confront us with how our lives might be adversely affecting others. Extending the notion of faith's privatization, we might conclude that the Ten Commandments and our obedience of them have also become privatized. We have turned them into our privatized moral codes without much consideration for the way they set forth a law that establishes who we have been created to be as human beings and the accountability and responsibility we have to each other and our life together as a human community.

The premise on which Luther's notions of obeying these commandments are based is simply this: obedience of these commandments has everything to do with trusting in the depths of our hearts that they are the very foundations for our life together as a human community, for how we live together, how we treat each other, and how we are able to have life, security and well being. They define who we have been created to be as human beings and how we are to live in human community with each other. They are the deep expression of God's merciful goodness and desire for human beings to have life. They are the directives that set forth what it

Living into Vocation

means to live in authentic human vocation under the cross. It's really quite simple: when these laws and commandments are trusted and followed, life works and functions as it was intended, and all human beings share in it equitably and peaceably. When they are not not trusted or followed, disastrous consequences follow, the powers of death and destruction take over and life as God desires and intends goes awry. In Luther's thinking, the Ten Commandments are not capricious laws, nor are they laws intended to be a burdensome weight that prevents the full embrace and enjoyment of life. Quite the opposite! They are laws that set God's directives and boundaries through which life is to be embraced, engaged, and enjoyed by the whole human community. When this foundational belief is trusted in the human heart, obedience follows. It's sounds simple enough, except we know it isn't.

At the risk of over simplifying the issue, an analogy through which we can better understand Luther's view of these commandments is to think about the laws that govern traffic and how we traverse from one location to another. Traffic laws exist for one purpose and one purpose only: to ensure that travel on streets and highways is safe, and that the lives of everyone traveling those roads is protected from harm and danger. That purpose, however, is based on an even deeper premise: the streets, roads, and highways that provide us pathways from one location to another are all shared equitably by everyone who travels them. It matters not who you are as a driver or a traveler. Your economic status does not matter, nor does the kind of vehicle you are driving matter. When you are on the road, you share it equitably with everyone else. No one on that road is more privileged or entitled to safety or access to the road than anyone else. All have a right to the road, and all who share that road together are accountable and responsible to protect the safety and life of each other. When any driver or traveler decides that the road is theirs to do with as they please or use it for their own purposes, we know the dangers that result. When the safety and lives of others no longer matter, chaos prevails and lives are placed in peril. All that matters to the rogue driver is the satisfaction of his own needs and desires, regardless of whether that desire is to satisfy his road rage and need for revenge, or his desire to have a thrill through reckless and careless driving. He is mindful of nothing other than the satisfaction of his own desires.

Safe driving that is attentive to the protection of others requires intentional mindfulness. On the highway, intentional mindfulness is an awareness that you are not the only person on the road and that the road is not yours to do with as you please. It is a vigilant awareness of all the laws that are applicable to your particular driving situation. It is a mindfulness that compels you to pay attention to your own physical condition and any limitations that might interfere with your ability to drive safely. More importantly, mindfulness is taking responsibility for your self and your behavior on the road so as to contribute to the safety and well being of everyone. It is generated and driven by a respect for the welfare of those with whom you share the road, and a belief and trust that the laws governing the road are there for everyone's safety, well-being, and protection. Obedience of traffic laws begins with a trust and mindfulness that they exist for a reason. And that reason is to insure that all have equitable access not only to the road, but to the safety and protection the laws are intended to provide. When this trust and belief is lost, disobedience will not be far behind.

When Mindfulness is Lost, Cancerous Behavior is Not Far Behind

I suggest that this idea of mindfulness is another way for us to hear the connection Luther makes between what is in our heart and how that translates into our outward behaviors toward others. It is another way for us to hear the prophetic voice in his instruction, for at every step of the way, Luther admonishes us to hear the extent to which the chief concern of each of these commandments is to protect our neighbor, ourselves, the human community, and the earth from the devilish and devastating harms that threaten life. When heard through the ears of love, they compel us to be mindful of who we have been created to be and the vocational purposes for which we were created. Without this kind of willful and intentional mindfulness, we become like rogue cancer cells that lose their ability to self-regulate and do nothing but heap harm and destruction on the cells and organisms around them.

In his book, *Failure of Nerve*, Edwin Friedman provides an excellent commentary on how the behaviors of cancer cells are identical and related to the rogue, aberrant and selfish behaviors of individuals and groups within organizational, communal and societal life.[1] Cells have the innate ability to differentiate themselves, develop a specialty, and organize themselves with cells that have a common purpose. Within the human body, brain cells organize themselves around the purpose of brain functioning, liver cells around liver functioning, muscular cells around muscular

---

1. Friedman, *Failure of Nerve*, 140–41.

functioning, and so forth. He also notes that healthy cells form into a community with common purpose—might we say vocation! They have the ability to communicate with each other and have a way of developing a network that "regulates each one's growth, behavior, and to some extent survival." Healthy cells have mindfulness. Cancer cells don't! They lose their capacity for self-differentiation, and they "remain permanently immature." They do not specialize, therefore, they cannot "colonize with a purpose that contributes to the organization of the larger community; the colonies that they do form (tumors) are totally un-self-regulating."[2] In other words, they lose their capacity for vocational purpose. They become rogues, reproducing uncontrollably, and subverting the body that gave them life. And unlike the healthy cells, these cancer cells do not know when to quit. Their inability to self-regulate means that they endlessly continue to inflict damage, destruction and death.

It does not take long to see how applicable Friedman's insight is to our present circumstances and the perils we face. The dehumanization, exploitation, power domination, and violence directed towards others are demonic, unregulated, and cancerous powers that bring harm and death to life. They are powers that obstruct a culture of life. Just as cancer cells stealthily invade the inner depths of our bodies to wreak their destruction without restraint, so do these cancerous behaviors invade our families, our communities, governments, nations, world, and yes our earth and environment, stealthily using our denial, illusions, and our willful twisting of reality to inflict their dastardly deeds!

And just as cancer cells do not come from a disease to which we have been exposed but are the result of unregulated cells being generated within, neither are our cancerous behaviors the result of exposure to an outside "disease." They are generated within the human community and within each of us by greed, hate, envy, and pride, and nurtured by the belief and value that the only thing that matters is personal self-satisfaction and gratification, regardless of who pays the price! They are so powerful that without our knowing it they turn us into cancer cells that have lost any sense of mindfulness., and in turn, cells that have lost vocational purpose. Turned into cancerous creatures, we inflict harm and danger onto others without our even knowing it. From Luther's perspective, that is precisely the reason these last seven commandments exist. In words written in his instruction

---

2. Friedman, *Failure of Nerve*, 140–41.

on the fifth commandment, but certainly extended to all of the last seven commandment, he says,

> God wants to have everyone defended, delivered, and protected from the wickedness and violence of others, and God has placed this commandment as a wall, fortress, and refuge around our neighbors so that no one may do them bodily harm or injury.[3]

That word, "harm," cannot be minimized, diminished or glossed over. Look in any dictionary or thesaurus and just about every word associated with harm would suggest and signify what Luther means: injury, hurt, pain, suffering, distress, anguish, trauma, torment, grief, damage, defacement, defilement, mischief, evil, badness, wrong, wrongdoing, immorality, wickedness, vice, iniquity, sin, sinfulness. All of a sudden, the reach of these commandments and what they are protecting extends significantly beyond our privatized world. They are no longer a moral list that is easily checked off with simple and cursory examinations of the obvious: "I haven't killed anyone;" "I haven't stepped out of my marriage;" "I haven't taken anything that doesn't belong to me," and so forth. Once again, Luther's instruction compels us to drill down and hear the questions that are being posed and put directly in front of us, questions that, if we are listening, will direct and lead us to "call a thing what it is." They awaken us to the ways we inflict harm on our neighbors, the world, and the earth when mindfulness gives way to self-absorbed and cancerous narcissism.

At the very center of Luther's instruction on these last seven commandments stands this one principle: like cells, we are all created with a vocational purpose, created to live and organize ourselves in ways that will serve the common good and ensure that all share equitably in life and its goodness. His instruction opens our eyes and ears to what it means to be authentic human beings who live in authentic human vocation, and what it means to be mindful of that vocation in all of our interactions with others; it is an instruction that calls us out of our privatized worlds to become and live into a culture of life that attends to the well being of neighbor and the human community. At the same time, it is an instruction that poignantly tells us of the harm and devastations we inflict on others when we lose our mindfulness and allow it to give way to our self-absorbed and narcissistic interests.

---

3. *TLC*, 328.

Living into Vocation

The Ten Commandments—Matters of the Heart

Luther understood the structure of the Ten Commandments to be rather straight forward. The first three have to do with how we are to relate to God; the last seven have to do with how we are to relate to each other as human beings in human community. The directives given in the first three commandments have to do with where we place our heart and trust for all of life, refuge, security and well being—God or mammon. If that is the case, then the directives of the last seven commandments concern themselves with how we physically and externally embody that heart outward in human community and in relationship with our neighbors.

Holding Neighbors in Our Heart

One of Jesus' most familiar parables is the parable of the Good Samaritan. As Luke recounts the story,[4] Jesus is asked by a lawyer to define, specifically and apparently in legal terms, just who his neighbor is. Instead of responding with legal verbiage, Jesus tells a story. A man is on the road from Jerusalem to Jericho. Along the way he encounters the perils of a band of robbers who beat him, take everything he has, and leave him for dead. A priest walks by, but after seeing the man and his condition he avoids the scene by walking on the other side. Another man walks by, a Levite, and he does the same thing. He avoids the scene by walking on the other side of the road. Then a Samaritan walks by. Remember Samaria? To the Jewish establishment, Samaria is the place of "otherness," and Samaritans are a people from borderland reality who are considered "other." Already, in his telling of this story, Jesus has turned the tables—a Samaritan offering empathic care to a Jew! As the story goes, the Samaritan's care does not end on the road. He takes the injured man to a nearby inn and instructs the innkeeper to attend to him as long as it takes for him to heal and recover. The Samaritan promises to return and cover the expenses.

The story concludes with Jesus asking the lawyer, "Of the three who passed by, who was the neighbor to the injured man?" Notice the question. It does not ask whether or not the injured man was a neighbor to the three that passed by. Rather it asks, of the three that passed by who was a neighbor to the injured man? Of course, what could the lawyer say but, "Well, I suppose it was the man who attended to the injured man." What made the

4. Luke 10:25–37, NRSV.

Samaritan the neighbor in this story is that he held the injured man in his heart. And just as importantly, what he held in his heart was embodied in his outward action of physically attending to the injured man's suffering and need. As much of an "other" and outsider as the Samaritan was, the life and well being of the injured man became as important to him as his own, if perhaps not more so.

I suggest that Luther's instruction on the last seven commandments regarding honoring parents and persons in authority, the taking of life, marriage, stealing, bearing false witness, and envious covetousness, all have to do with how we hold our neighbors in our heart—or don't. On the surface, each of these commandments appear to be commandments of prohibition, don't do this, don't do that. And Luther's explanations can sound just like that: don't do this or don't do that. Yet, there is something beyond what is seen on the surface that awakens us to the commandment's deeper meaning. And that deeper meaning will always have to do with holding our neighbor's welfare in our heart and embodying that heart in our external and physical actions.

Holding Those Entrusted To Us In Our Hearts

Let's be honest, Luther's instruction on the fourth commandment is difficult to comprehend and interpret in our own context. Upon reading it, one wonders how his instruction can be taken seriously or followed at all, given its very strict and narrow language on the obedience of authority, whether that authority is parental, spiritual or governmental. Ours is a society replete with child abuse and neglect. A day does not go by without hearing a story about a child being abused, whether it be by parents, school teachers, priests, or ministers. Moreover, the news is filled with story after story about governmental leaders and persons in authority taking advantage of their office for personal gain. With the treatment many cultural and ethnic minorities have received from law enforcement and other civil authorities—the killings of Ahmaud Aubrey, George Floyd and other Black Americans, the detention of undocumented Latiné immigrants and separation of children from their parents—public respect for police and civil authority, at least among ethnic and cultural minorities, has eroded. With the revelations of child sexual abuse cases among Roman Catholic priests, and overt sexual misconduct among clergy in general, how do we come to terms with Luther's instruction that priests, pastors, and ministers are our "spiritual parents?" How do we

Living into Vocation

come to terms with Luther's admonition to respect, honor and obey parents because they are "God's representatives" when for many, parental behavior towards their children is dysfunctional at best and criminal at worst? Moreover, Luther's statements that persons in positions of subservient servitude to their masters should be happy and thankful that they have employment, give thanks for what they have, and obey their masters with a joyful heart smacks of nothing more than assigning to them a God-given place in life out of which they have no possible alternatives.

The fact is, Luther lived in a European medieval feudal system where clear hierarchical and class distinctions between lords, their vassals, and their servants were normative, and even seen as the way God ordained societal order. While it is helpful to understand this societal structure as the world to which Luther was addressing his instruction, that is not the world we live in. Obviously, ours is a culture vastly separated and vastly different from the hierarchical, feudal, world of Luther. Moreover, we are the beneficiaries of considerable knowledge on human behavior, child development, not to mention the beneficiaries of the knowledge we have gained about predatory behaviors. In the face of all the awakenings this knowledge has given us, it would seem reasonable to disregard Luther's instruction on this commandment altogether.

Reading and meditating on the *Large Catechism* is like looking at a hologram. If you stay focused on the image you see on the surface, you completely miss the image that lies underneath. And so it is with this commandment. The instruction that lies below the surface speaks directly to the abusive, oppressive, and dehumanizing behaviors that parents inflict on their children, and the exploitative behaviors persons in authority and care have inflicted on those who have been entrusted to them for nurture, protection, and education.

Luther's instruction on the honor and respect that should be given to parents and persons in authority is predicated on one foundational premise: parents and persons who are in positions of authority are persons to whom the lives of others have been entrusted for their care and well being. This entrustment is not perfunctory or superficial. It is a matter of the heart! When the life of another is entrusted to me for their care and well being, what happens to their life becomes as important to me as what happens to my own life. When someone's life is entrusted to me, I am literally being given the responsibility to carry that person's welfare and well being in my heart, and to embody that care in my actions towards that person whose life has been entrusted to me. Conversely, when I know that someone is carrying me in their heart, that they truly care about my life and what happens to me, even when they confront or reprimand me, I trust that they have my well being at heart. It is that trust that engenders my respect, and my willingness to receive their admonitions. This I suggest is what lies below the surface of Luther's instruction on the fourth commandment. One might actually say that while his words are directed to children and anyone under the authority of someone else, they are actually and more directly pointed at those to whom the lives of others have been entrusted for care and well being. Hear his words:

> Everyone acts as if God gave us children for our pleasure and amusement, gave us servants merely to put to work as cows or donkeys, and gave us subjects to treat as we please, as if it were not concern of ours what they learn or how they live. No one is willing to see that this is the command of the divine Majesty who will solemnly call us to account and punish us for its neglect.[5]

We can interpolate this to mean that children or any person whose life has been entrusted to us are not objects to be used or manipulated to serve our demands or serve our purposes. Rather they are human beings whose lives are to be held in our heart. To hold children or persons who are under our supervision, authority or governance in our heart is to care about what happens to them as much as we care about what happens to us; it is to care enough that we care about their future and who or what they become as human beings.

Bringing this into our own context, we turn to the noted educator and author, Parker Palmer. In his book, *The Courage to Teach*, Palmer speaks to the powerful learning that comes when a teacher holds students in her heart. He writes, "The connections made by good teachers are held not in their methods but in their hearts—meaning *heart* in its ancient sense, as the place where intellect, emotion, and spirit will converge in the human self."[6]

Palmer's point is simply this. When teachers hold students in their hearts, a deep connection is made, a connection in which they are joined with the student in such a way that they themselves become vulnerable to feeling the humanness of the student. He goes on:

---

5. *TLC*, 326.
6. Palmer, *Courage to Teach*, 11.

> Small wonder, then, that teaching tugs at the heart, opens the heart, even breaks the heart—and the more one loves teaching, the more heartbreaking it can be. The courage to teach is the courage to keep one's heart open in those very moments when the heart is asked to hold more than it is able so that teacher and students and subject can be woven into the fabric of community that learning, and living, require.[7]

I suggest that Palmer's words can be applied to any position where persons, whether parents or persons in authority of any kind, have been entrusted with the lives of others for their care, safety, and well being, and entrusted with the responsibility to help them develop into human beings who will live in the world with the capability of opening their own hearts to the welfare and good of others. All human beings, whether children or adults, cannot open their hearts to hold the hearts of others unless their own heart has been held, cared for, and loved. And that, I suggest, is the core of Luther's instruction on the fourth commandment: persons to whom the lives of others have been entrusted are to be mindful of what they have been entrusted with, mindful of the vocational responsibilities that this entrustment entails, mindful of what they have been given to carry in their heart.

In a powerful article titled, "When a Heart is Empty," David Brooks, commentator and op ed writer for *The New York Times,* makes this powerful observation:

> I see less and less of this attention in America (referring to the opening of heart and the capacity to carry the pain and suffering of others), even after the tragedies of 2020. Far from softening to one another, the whole country feels even more rived, more hardened, and increasingly blind to lives other than our own.[8]

Luther's instruction on the fourth commandment is a needed prophetic word for these difficult and perilous times, as Brooks' and Palmer's words so clearly attest! We know from these past years what happens to a society and community when the hearts of parents become focused on themselves and hardened to the needs of others; we also know how this gets transmitted to children, and then beyond. We know ever so clearly what happens to our government when its leaders become self-absorbed into their own interests and ideologies, closing their hearts to the sufferings and needs of those they serve. We know all too well what happens to the earth

---

7. Palmer, *Courage to Teach,* 11.
8. Brooks, "When a Heart is Empty," Lines 76–80.

when our hearts turn to the gratification of our own cravings at the expense of its life giving resources. The list could go on. There is no easy answer to any of these predicaments. But one thing is clear: as Christians and followers of Jesus, our "office" and vocation is to teach our children and those who follow us—by word and example—how to soften and open our hearts to the plights and sufferings of their neighbors, community, world, and the earth. When we are mindful of this vocational office, we will begin to be a culture of life that resists the cancerous behaviors of death. With this mindfulness, we and those who follow us will become what Luther described as "little Christs" to the world!

You Shall Not Passively Stand By When Harm Is Being Inflicted on Your Neighbor

Throughout this discussion, we have asserted that the powers of death are closer than we think. To be sure, these powers are present in the obvious—gun violence, domestic terrorism, random shootings, and acts of domestic violence to name but a few. But they are also present in the dehumanization, exploitation, and power domination that takes place in racism, white supremacy, global warming and abuse of the earth, economic injustice, disparity between the rich and the poor, and the list could go on. These powers are not only present, they are actively at work and in our face, threatening and bringing harm to multitudes of the world's population. One only need to look around at the devastations being endured by the countless victims of racial hate, the victims of destruction of wildfires and catastrophic hurricanes, the increasing numbers of homeless and hungry people who are left to find rest and food on the streets, and again the list could go on.

The fact is, none of these deathly powers just happen. They are the result of the greed, lust, pride, and self-absorbed indulgence of a few, the harmful effects of which have been heaped upon the many, mostly the poor, marginalized, and disenfranchised. Yet in the face of these powers and the harms they are inflicting, we seem numbed, paralyzed, or unwilling to do anything about it. In our affluent and self-absorbed culture, we seem content to stand by, passively feeling pity or even offering our prayers for the victims of these powers, yet not all that motivated to carry them in our hearts in such a way that we would stand with them to defend and assist them to resist the harms and threats these powers are inflicting.

While Luther's explication to the fifth commandment is a clear prohibition against any physical act of violence, he expands its scope by saying that the Christian's obligation is to be proactive in defending or assisting one's neighbor against any harm that would threaten their life. In rather direct words, Luther asserts that

> ... this commandment is violated not only when we do evil, but also when we have the opportunity to do good to our neighbors and to prevent, protect, and save them from suffering bodily harm or injury but fail to do so ... It will be of no help for you to use the excuse that you did not assist their deaths by world or deed, for you have withheld your love from them and robbed them of the kindness by which their lives might have been saved.[9]

As harsh as it may sound, standing by in passive silence and watching our neighbor suffer and endure the harms inflicted by another's behavior without offering solidarity or assistance is a matter of withholding our love. In Luther's instruction, this is as much a violation of this commandment as the perpetration of a violent physical act. Let's be clear. There are plenty of caring and charitable people who witness to their love through the help and assistance they offer those who have been harmed by natural disasters and other catastrophes. Theirs is, by all means, a good work. But Luther is talking about something more than charitable giving. I suggest that in our present context, the application of his instruction has everything to do with how we respond—or fail to respond—to the harms that are being inflicted on others as a result of our self-absorbed greed, lust, pride, and envy, the harms of dehumanization, exploitation, and power domination. We are quite content to make our charitable contributions, all of which are good; yet we seem reluctant, if not unwilling, to engage in the more risky actions of standing in solidarity with our neighbors to defend and assist them when they are the victims of injustice and other threatening harms.

In this regard, I refer back to the vignette of the church community's reaction when an anti-racism statement was presented not long after the Ahmaud Arbery killing. You will recall that the statement was drafted with the intent of calling on congregations to engage in conversations on racism with the intent of challenging them to increase their awareness of racism's presence in their communities and to embark on the work of dismantling racism and its threats. One reactive comment suggested that the statement was "hostile," while other reactions simply indicated that their

9. *TLC*, 329.

congregations would not likely be willing to undertake such a conversation. On the surface, it may not seem as though these reactions have anything to do with Luther's admonition about coming to the aid of our neighbors when they are threatened by harm. Yet, I suggest that these reactive comments are indications of the very passive silence and withholding of love to which Luther referred in his instruction on the fifth commandment. It is a passive silence that makes us active and complicit partners in the harm that has been or is being perpetrated.

Understandably, any conversation whose purpose is to gain an awareness of what racism is and of its presence in ourselves and our communities is disquieting and unsettling. The resistance to engaging it is understandable. Even more understandable is the question most would raise, "How can the engagement of such an unsettling conversation actually help, defend, and assist persons upon whom the harms of racism have been inflicted? I return to the story of Allison and me. Until I was willing to open my eyes and ears to the dynamics that were present in the room—a perspective that she saw but my self-perceptions and illusions did not allow me to see—I was unable to stand with her in a partnership and solidarity that would empower both of us to resist the racism and power domination that existed in the room. Until I shifted my position, we could not change. The only way out of these self-perceptions and illusion was to open myself to see things through her eyes, a step that was not easy to make, yet one that turned out to be life giving for both of us.

This is the very encounter of which we spoke earlier, the encounter with the "otherness" of those who are different from ourselves. Stepping out of our comfortable safety zones to cross the thresholds of our unregulated fear into a conversation that may cause unsettling dis-ease is to take the risky step towards obedience. I suggest it is the necessary step towards the kind of obedience and proactivity of which Luther speaks in his instruction on the fifth commandment.

You Shall Honor the Vocation of Marriage

Let's be honest. Human relationships at any level are complex, and in moments of stress, anxiety, or conflict they can be difficult to navigate and maintain. At the same time, we know them to be a vital source of emotional, physical, and spiritual life giving energy. We cannot live without them. This being the case, the relationship between two human beings that

Living into Vocation

evolves into the life long and intimate commitment of marriage is even more difficult. We also know, though, that the intimate bond of a marital union, regardless of how two people come into it, can be a rich source of vitality, renewal, joy, inspiration, and life giving energy. It is no wonder that persons of faith have considered the marital union and bond to be holy, in spite of its complexities and difficulties.

Relationships at any level cannot be taken for granted, as if they will somehow sustain themselves on their own. They require nurture and sustentation if they are to maintain their durability and capacity to be a source of life giving energy. For the marital relationship and union, this requirement is even greater. From the time they enter their marital commitment, couples are already vulnerable to the threat of divorce. And what is it that makes the marital union so vulnerable? While there are many contributing factors, I suggest that one is the very issue we have noted throughout this whole discussion: our affluent, narcissistic culture's focus on self-gratification and the immediate satisfaction of one's needs, wants, and desires. With such focus on the primacy of the self, our capacity to give ourselves to another without thought of what we will get in return is greatly diminished. To use traditional Christian marital language, our capacity *to become one with another* has been greatly impaired.

In this section, I want to address how Luther's instruction on the sixth commandment is more than a prohibition against sexual impropriety; it is an instruction on living in the vocation of marriage. But first, I share a story to help illustrate the issue we are addressing.

The story is of a couple I came to know early in ministry as they came for pastoral help with issues in their marriage. Both were professionals and their positions made them visible and interactive with the community. On the surface their relationship appeared good and stable. However as I came to know them, I realized that the wife was unhappy, and at times even depressed. In time, I realized that this woman was a brilliant and intelligent woman. She had been at the top of her high school graduating class, yet after two year of college, she left to marry and follow her husband in his chosen career. Although she later returned to finish her degree and obtain a position in their community, her unhappiness and depression remained. While the dynamics of their marital relationship were more complex than this brief narrative can detail, it became clear that an important contribution to their difficulties was the extent to which he wanted her to be what he expected rather than that she live in the authenticity of her own humanness. Given this, her own brilliant intelligence, and her identity as a woman with her own strengths and gifts lived in the shadows of his career. Her role in the marital union was to be his supportive wife at the expense of her own authenticity. On more than one occasion, I observed that his public displays of affection were often patronizing, sounding as though he was talking to a little girl. When hearing her constructive but negative feedback to his public presentations, he would react with either anger or sulkiness. In his own insecurity, he was dependent on her for his own identity and security, and it was a dependency that suppressed and oppressed her ability to communicate and relate to him out of her own authentic self. Eventually the role into which she had been slotted, and from which she felt she could not escape resulted in the demise of her physical and emotional health. She separated from him for a period of time, and I suspect that during this separation, she might have engaged in an extra-marital relationship. She eventually returned, but it was never clear that they ever found healing or health in their marital union.

Like with all of Luther's explication of the last seven commandments, his instruction on this commandment is intended to prevent harm from being inflicted on the marital relationship and the marriage partners. To be sure, the harm to which Luther refers is the harm that comes when one of the partners engages in a sexual relationship outside of the boundaries of the marital union, or the harm that is possibly inflicted on another relationship by the same action. The point of this illustration is that in this marriage, harms were inflicted long before their was a separation and long before there was any possibility of extramarital sexual activity. More to the point, I am suggesting that Luther's instruction is challenging us to look beyond our narrow purviews that tell us this commandment is solely about prohibiting sexual impropriety. Rather it is posing us with the more complex questions of how harm is inflicted on our partner or the marriage itself when we lose our mindfulness and regard for the integrity and dignity of our partner, or when our partner becomes merely an object intended to satisfy and meet our own needs and desires.

Luther was quite clear that fidelity and faithfulness to the sexual intimacy of a marriage is something that cannot happen unless the foundations of self-giving love are present. Indeed, it is but an outgrowth of that love's presence. Hear his words:

> ...this commandment requires all people not only to live chastely in deed, word, and thought in their particular situation (especially

in marriage as a walk of life), but also to love and cherish the spouse whom God has given them. Wherever marital chastity is to be maintained, above all it is essential that husbands and wives (partners) live together in love and harmony, cherishing each other wholeheartedly and with perfect fidelity. This is one of the chief ways to make chastity attractive and desirable. Under such conditions, chastity always follows spontaneously without any command.[10]

As I hope the illustration above makes clear, the powers of self-absorbed narcissism are the barriers and obstructions that prevent us from being able to cherish, honor, and give thanks to God for the gift of our marital partner. In a world of self-absorption and self-gratification where the world revolves around "me," I want others to be who I want and need them to be, not who they really are. How can I cherish who they are if they have to meet my expectation of being who I want them to be? In my narcissism, I cannot see or love the other for who they are, either in their goodness or their brokenness. I can only see them through the eyes of who or what I want or need them to be. When Luther speaks of inflicting no harm upon marriage or spouse, it is not just the harm that comes when one has stepped out of the sexual boundaries of marriage. It's the harm that comes when one or the other in the marital bond turns the other into an object to serve their needs and wants without mindful regard or respect for what the other might need or want from them. Harm is inflicted when our mindfulness gives way to self-absorption and self-centeredness.

True love in a marriage breaks the barriers of superficiality, fantasies, and illusions. It sees the other for who they are, their frailties, their goodness and their brokenness. Not only does it see the other for who they are, it takes the risk of committing and entrusting one's self, life and well being to them, and to having them entrust their life to you. It risks encountering them and being encountered by them! This is human vocation, the vocation for which all human beings are created, and it is the vocation of marriage, or marriage's "walk of life," as Luther called it.[11]

For Luther the vocation of marriage is not only for the sake of the two marriage partners. Like the culture of a starter that affects everything with which it is mixed, the culture of life that is seeded in the marital union extends into the world and the relationships to which we belong by virtue

10. *TLC*, 335.
11. *TLC*, 332–35.

of its being part and parcel of the human community. Think of the marriage relationship as a microcosm of how God wants all human beings to treat each other: not as objects who exist to serve the other's self-interests, self-preoccupations, self-gratifications or self-pursuits, but rather as fellow human beings who exist to help each and empower each other to grow into the fulness of their humanity and their own human vocations. Dorothy Day, the now deceased American Catholic social activist and journalist says it ever so well:

> True love is delicate and kind, full of gentle perception and understanding, full of beauty and grace, full of joy unutterable. There should be some flavor of this in all our love for others. We are all one. We are one flesh in the Mystical Body as man and woman are said to be one flesh in marriage. With such a love one would see all things new; we would begin to see people as they really are, as God sees them.[12]

This is indeed the holy vocation of marriage. As Luther said,

> Married life is no matter for jest or idle curiosity, but it is a glorious institution and an object of God's serious concern. For it is of utmost importance to God that persons be brought up to serve the world, promote knowledge of God, godly living, and all virtues and to fight against wickedness and the devil (evil).[13]

And what is it to serve the world and to promote God, justice, and to resist evil but to be a culture of life that will empower human beings to live with each other in the true authenticity of their humanness. This is indeed the vocation of marriage to which God wants no harm to be inflicted.

You Shall Not Steal or Take Advantage of Another

The idea of using others to serve our own desires and wants extends into the seventh commandment, you shall not steal. It is a commandment, Luther asserted, intended to prevent the harm that comes when our lives are invaded and disrupted by those who are intent to take what doesn't belong to them, those who by robbery, theft, larceny, or scam want to put money, property, and power into their own hands and pockets without any regard for what those actions will do to their victims.

12. Day, "83 Notable Quotes."
13. *TLC*, 332.

Living into Vocation

A few years ago when travel was part of my job, I was awakened in my hotel room by a phone call. I answered, half asleep. The person on the other end claimed to be from the hotel's front desk, telling me that a computer malfunction had occurred and that my credit card information had been lost. The person then asked me for my credit card number so that it could be used for my charges. Half asleep and caught off guard, I didn't think, so I gave my number. Within a minute or two after hanging up and coming to my senses, I realized what had happened. I was the victim of a scam, a scam which I quickly learned had occurred throughout the hotel. Without question, I should've been much more vigilant, cautious, and non-compliant. But I wasn't. And that's the point. We live in a culture where the desire to make easy money or acquire more wealth and power leads many to prey and take advantage of the unsuspecting, the vulnerable, the innocent, and the gullible. And without question, my unsuspecting, naive, and half awakened brain were taken advantage of. By the time I had come to my senses, my card had already been used for about two hundred dollars worth of purchases, all of which I was able to have returned once I called the credit card company. Regardless, I was taken advantage of.

But this is the point of Luther's explanation to the seventh commandment:

> . . . to steal is nothing else than to acquire someone else's property by unjust means. These few words include taking advantage of our neighbor in any sort of dealings that result in loss to them . . . stealing is not just robbing someone's safe or pocketbook but also taking advantage of someone in the market, in all stores, butcher shops, wine and beer cellars, workshops, and, in short, wherever business is transacted and money is exchanged for goods and services.[14]

Compared to the many other forms the taking advantage of others has in the world, the hotel scam to which I just referred was minor. It was rectified quickly. Think, though, of the white collar crimes where persons investing for retirement end up losing everything—as in Enron and the Bernie Madoff Ponzi schemes, to name only two. The FBI notes that corporate fraud remains one of its highest priorities because of the damage it inflicts not only on individual investors, but the damage it can inflict on an entire economy.[15] One can see the extent to which individual greed leads to a dehumanizing exploitation of the unsuspecting and vulnerable in the

14. *TLC,* 335.
15. "White Collar Crime," *FBI.*

form of deceptive theft. More pernicious and harmful is that those who have committed such theft have violated the sacred trust that was given to them when people entrusted their money—their life!—to them. And therein lies the core of Luther's instruction on this commandment. When people are taken advantage of by others, those who are taken advantage of are being dehumanized, and exploited to serve the greed of those who have taken whatever was entrusted to them. Anytime trust is violated, dehumanization, denigration, and exploitation have occurred.

But thievery in the form of taking advantage of others occurs beyond corporate or investment fraud. Who is being taken advantage of when 5 percent of the world's population, the United States, uses 24 percent of the earth's resources to support its consumeristic and materialistic life style? Who is being taken advantage of when the 20 percent of the world's population who are its wealthiest use 76.6 percent of its resources for their life styles, while the remaining 80 percent use only 23.4 percent? A comment that sits alongside this data on the Washington State University website states the extent and enormity of this consumeristic thievery:

> Reducing consumption without reducing use is a costly delusion. If undeveloped countries consumed at the same rate as the US, four complete planets the size of the Earth would be required. People who think that they have a right to such a life are quite mistaken.[16]

Extending the notion of who is taking advantage of who, and for what reasons, we can ask who is being taken advantage of when "cheap labor" is used as a means of making products and goods more affordable and available for our affluent consumer driven life styles? Who is being taken advantage of when price gouging occurs for the basics of life after natural disasters? Who or what is being taken advantage of when the earth's forests are being deforested at an alarming rate to satisfy our appetites for beef and other agricultural products, or when other natural resources are blatantly used without consideration of who is being affected or taken advantage of? You get the point. In a narcissistic and self-absorbed culture where greed, envy, pride and hate lead to exploitation, dehumanization, and power domination, we are usually not mindful of who or what is being affected or taken advantage of by our desire and need to satisfy our consumeristic, self-serving appetites and need for power. More to the point, we are not mindful nor do we seem to care that our silent and passive response to these kinds

---

16. Washington State University, "Consumption in America."

of harmful activities actually makes us a complicit participant in them. When we begin to see the scope of how one group of human beings takes advantage of another group of human beings, or one group uses its power to deprive another group of its rights we can understand Luther's words:

> In short, thievery is the most common craft and the largest guild on earth. If we look at the whole world in all its situations, it is nothing but a big, wide stable full of great thieves. This is why these people are also called armchair bandits and highway robbers. Far from being pickpockets and sneak thieves who pilfer the cash box, they sit in their chairs and are known as great lords and honorable, upstanding citizens, while they rob and steal under the cloak of legality.[17]

You Shall Not Bear False Witness

One might well argue that of all the commandments, the eighth commandment, you shall not bear false witness against your neighbor, has become one of the most relevant in our present context. Of all the ills and devastations that surround us, one of the most threatening is the pernicious assault on truth, an assault that is taking place at all levels of our life together. To be sure, truth is hard to pin down. What appears to be the truth of a situation or predicament to one person will not be so for someone else. Different perceptions of a matter lead to different tellings of what was true. But in our present moment, we are talking about something that is quite different from having varying perspectives on an issue. The present assault on truth has to do with deliberate and malicious lies that are construed and broadcast with the purposeful intent of distorting reality and turning that reality into something that it never was and that facts have not substantiated or proven. Moreover, it is the construction and broadcasting of lies that have the intent of destroying persons' careers, reputations, and integrity.

Luther understood that one's personal integrity and reputation were as critical to life as were all of its basic necessities. He said:

> Besides our own body, our spouse, and our temporal property, we have one more treasure that is indispensable to us, namely our honor and good reputation. For it is important that we not live among people in public disgrace and dishonor. Therefore God does not want our neighbors deprived of their reputation, honor,

---

17. *TLC,* 337.

and character any more than of their money and possessions; God wants everyone to maintain self respect before spouse, child, servant and neighbor.[18]

Consider the importance of that word, self-respect. At its core, self-respect has everything to do with how one views one's self as a human being. To have self-respect is to perceive one's self as a valued human being and a contributing participant in the human community. To lose one's self-respect or to have it taken away is to be shamed into feeling less than human. While not a physical death, it is nevertheless a form of death, for anytime one has been shamed into feeling less than human, a death has occurred within their spirit and soul. With the rise of social media as a venue for public discourse, the ability to inflict dangerous harm on another through the telling of lies or the distortion of factual information has increased significantly. It is a phenomenon that has come to be defined as *internet shaming*. In a blog on the resource website, Tech Target, the website's content editor, Ivy Wigmore, says that,

> Internet shaming is the use of social media, blogs and other online communication channels to attack a target individual or organization. The purpose of the attack is often to publicly embarrass the target, often as retribution for some behavior.[19]

She went on to suggest that while some online shaming can be a form of vigilantism intended to take matters of justice into their own hands, it is also used as a means of spite, retribution, or simply a means to discredit and devalue the one who is being attacked. The problem she noted is that online communication is volatile. It is instantaneous and therefore, "the immediacy of response also means that those sharing messages may send them before checking facts and giving the matter due consideration."[20] Moreover, they turn into vicious attacks. The demonic power of these attacks is evidenced in that fact that they have "led to threats, physical attacks, lost jobs, disruption of families and suicides."[21] The telling and disseminating of deceitful lies and untruths are nothing less than an attempt to exercise power and control over others. To take away the self-respect of another human being is to exercise a power that is dehumanizing in its most despicable

---

18. *TLC*, 341.
19. Wigmore, "Internet Shaming," lines 1–3.
20. Wigmore, "Internet Shaming," lines 11–14.
21. Wigmore, "Internet Shaming," line 18.

form. It is to reduce them to a less than human object. And as with any act of dehumanization or power domination, the one who inflicts the harm has viewed himself as a god who somehow thinks he has the right and power to make or break another human being. It is a right and power that comes with feeling entitled and self-justified.

One would have thought that Luther was writing to our age of online and digital communication when he said that this commandment

> applies to all of us, forbids all sins of the tongue by which we may injure or offend our neighbor. "Bearing false witness" is nothing but a work of the tongue. God wants to hold in check whatever is done with the tongue against a neighbor . . . It applies especially to the detestable, shameless vice of backbiting or slander by which the devil rides us. To avoid this vice, therefore, we should note that none of us has the right to judge and reprove a neighbor publicly, even after having seen a sin committed . . . There is a great difference between judging a sin and having knowledge of a sin. You may certainly know about a sin, but you should not judge it.[22]

The demonic power of vengeful words can be as powerful as life threatening weapons. The harm inflicted is not fleeting or easily removed. As Luther observed, ". . . honor and good name are easily taken away, but not easily restored."[23] Even, when the harm is inflicted through the venue of social media.

As the political landscape of our country has revealed in these past several years, the intentional telling and disseminating of lies and untruths is a ploy to exercise political power by preying on people's angry sentiments and feelings of vulnerabilities. It is nothing less than an attempt at power domination. More devastating is its demonic intent to destroy the very fabric that holds a country and democracy together, namely truth and trust. We have seen this in the lies that were propagated and spread about the 2020 election, a lie that was conceived and spread even before the election was held, thus casting a doubt in the minds of many that the election would be invalid before it was even held. As it turned out, the voices that promulgated and disseminated that lie grew louder, even as they could not prove in any court of law that the election was fraudulent. In their power lust, and in the power lust of those who believed and placed their hope in what those lies offered them, the lie became a reality even when it was proven to have

---

22. *TLC,* 343.
23. *TLC,* 344.

had no factual basis. It is a lie that sowed mistrust and contempt for the long held and long trusted constitutional process of casting and counting votes. It is a lie that has led some states to create laws that will restrict and even deny some voters their right to vote. If one thinks that this is a political matter that should be kept out of a discussion on matters of faith, hear what Luther said of the eighth commandment:

> The first application of this commandment, then, is that all people should help their neighbors maintain their legal rights. One must not allow these rights to be thwarted or distorted, but should promote and resolutely guard them, whether this person is judge or witness, no matter what the consequences may be.[24]

While Luther's application is directed towards protecting our neighbor's legal rights from witnesses' deceptive lies in a court of law, the idea that our neighbor's legal rights should be guarded and protected from the deceitful lies that seek to deprive or lessen those rights in any way is unmistakably clear. In a political climate such as ours, where intentional lies that have no factual basis are pronounced on a regular basis with the sole intent of gaining political power or destroying another's reputation and life, the dehumanization of and the power domination over others has taken precedent over the common good. To guard against the harm that is inflicted on our neighbors from willful and deceitful lies is not only a protection of our neighbor's integrity and self-respect as a human being, it is to protect our life together as a human community from those who would destroy the very fabric of what holds us together—truth and trust.

You Shall Not Covet Anything That Is Your Neighbor's

In his explanation to the ninth and tenth commandments, Luther calls out and exposes the screens and cover ups that upstanding and honorable people use to commit acts of thievery. The screen behind which culprits hide their unethical and rogue behavior, he said, is civil law. Hear his words:

> . . . the seventh commandment prohibits seizing or withholding someone else's possession to which you have no right. But here it is also forbidden to entice anything away from your neighbor, even

---

24. *TLC*, 342.

though in the eyes of the world you could do it honorably, without accusation or blame for fraudulent gain.[25]

He goes on:

> Everyone tries to accumulate as much as one can and let others look out for themselves. Yet we all consider ourselves persons with integrity and put up a fine front to conceal our villainy. We hunt for and think up clever tricks and shrewd tactics . . . under the guise of justice. We brazenly dare to boast of it and defiantly insist that it should not be called rascality but shrewdness and foresight. In this we are abetted by jurists and lawyers who twist and stretch the law to suit their purpose, straining words and using them for pretexts without regard for equity or for our neighbor's plight. In short, whoever is sharpest and shrewdest in such matters gets most advantage out of the law . . .[26]

In other words, the fact that an action is legal or even appears to be legal does not make that action right, ethical or just. Luther's words, "Everyone tries to accumulate as much as one can and let others look out for themselves," takes us back to the very first commandment regarding idolatry and where we place our heart. The one who places his heart on the acquisition of wealth and property has no mindfulness or concern for what his selfishness is doing to another human being. All that matters is satisfying his entitled greed.

Consistent with this discussion's assertion that Luther's instruction on these commandments is like a hologram where there is always something below the surface, the "something that is below the surface" in these two commandments is narcissism's self-absorbed sense of entitlement that leads to a complete loss of mindfulness which in turn leads to a complete loss of boundaries. In short, what Luther is getting at is our inability to regulate ourselves, our desires, and our cravings, an inability that results in envious and covetous behaviors with no mindfulness as to who might be affected.

So what drives this absence of mindfulness? It is the same thing driving all of our behaviors that bring harm to our neighbor regardless of who they are and where they are located. It is the inability to discern and regulate our feelings of entitled wants, desires, and privileges. This inability to discern and self-regulate feelings and behaviors is in individuals, in corporations, and in our cultural mind set. Think about it. The action of trying to take

25. *TLC*, 349.
26. *TLC*, 349.

over something we want but doesn't belong to us is driven by a belief that we are entitled to act on our feelings. If I *feel* I want something, I am entitled to act on those feelings without regard or deference to how that action will harm someone else. If we *feel* we need a resource to produce a product or commodity to satisfy our desires and wants, we are usually not much concerned about how our acquisition of that resource will affect the country or people who own that resource. We want it, therefore, we will find a way to acquire it regardless of who is impacted by the acquisition. This deeply felt entitlement erodes and eats away at whatever boundaries we may have. The need to do violence or take the life of another is driven by the feeling and desire for revenge and a belief that I am entitled to act on my feelings; I am entitled to the revenge and the satisfaction getting even will give me. I am entitled to see that whoever did me wrong is repaid. The same entitlement comes into play when it comes to matters of sexual intimacy. I am entitled to act on my feelings of lust without regard to the effect or harm that may bring to another or to a marriage! I am entitled to pleasure, satisfaction and gratification regardless of who is hurt. The same entitlement drives thievery, whether it is the thievery of so called thugs, or the thievery of well groomed persons of business; it is the belief that I am entitled to act on my desires to have what I want, regardless of the harm it inflicts.

But that's the way self-absorbed narcissism works. It has no mindfulness for others, no room for matters of the heart, no room or concern for the feelings of others or how one's actions will affect another, the losses or the sufferings they will encounter. The inability to discern and regulate feelings is an underhanded and malicious cancer that goes undetected, yet brings considerable harm to the one who has been impacted. This by no means suggests that one's feelings should be ignored. Feelings are a gift of God and cannot be ignored. But they must be discerned, because without discernment and regulation, they can become the tool of our self-absorbed narcissism. They can become the tool that detracts and takes us out of vocation into a survival mode of living!

Living in Contradictions with Hope

From the gospel's perspective—and the *Large Catechism*'s—the one characteristic that defines humanity and human beings apart from the world of self-absorbed narcissism is that each and every human being, regardless of race, ethnicity, religion, color, or culture, is but one life giving organism

Living into Vocation

among many, ordained with the purpose of functioning in such a way that the whole human community will benefit and have life. When one or a group of organisms goes into survival mode and tries in and of itself to be the whole body or the center of the body without any regard to the interdependency that holds them all together, the human community and creation are threatened. The commandments are intended to be the laws that hold all human community together, laws that direct the functioning of every human being so that all of humanity, and all of creation become what they were created for and intended. Yes, it sounds like a nice ideal and a dream. Except it isn't. It is the *real world* into which the gospel calls us to live, move, and have our being, the real world of which we are to be mindful in every interaction and intersection of our life. It is the real world of living in a vocation under the cross.

It is not hard to recognize the inconsistencies and contradictions that exist between the vocational purposes for which we were created and the extent to which our cancerous behaviors have led us away from those purposes. We are not who we might have thought ourselves to be. Luther's instruction on the commandments make very clear the contradictions that exist between what we were created to be and who and what we are not. It is not hard to recognize that we have gone astray and awry from the lives for which we were intended and created. It is not hard to recognize just how broken the human community is. We know how close death really is, and we know how much our own behaviors have contributed to our being in this place.

However, while these commandments starkly reveal what we are not, they also set forth the vision of the human beings and the human community we are becoming in our dying and rising with Christ. They are the vision of the new creation and the new vocation which God is calling forth in our baptism. They are the vision of God's future and the authentic humanity to which our lives are now and presently directed by our baptism, even if faintly. They confront us with the truth of the contradictions and negations of our life; yet, at the very same time, they are the vision and directives of the vocation into which we are becoming. We are not left in a place of hopeless despair or a place of no way out. As Black slaves so well expressed, it is in the cross of Jesus the Christ that God has provided "a way out of no way," a way into God's hope-filled future!

For Luther, the radical good news of the gospel is that in death's power over life and even God's apparent abandonment of life, God is mysteriously present, creating and bringing forth life out of hopeless death. It is precisely in this liminal place that our baptism takes on meaning and importance. For if it is that our baptism has joined us to Jesus' dying and rising, then it is in these moments of hopeless dying that we are actually and at the very same time being raised and created into a new creation and a new human community with vocational purpose. That is the mystery of faith we declare in every celebration of the Eucharist, "*Christ has died, Christ has risen, Christ will come again.*" This is not just an affirmation about Jesus the Christ. It is an affirmation of of our baptism and the future into which we are living. It is an affirmation of the baptismal vocation into which we are being called and created. In that affirmation of faith's mystery, we affirm the power of God's future in the face of death and all of its powers. Yes, even in the face of the powers of our self-absorbed narcissism! It is a future that is already near and among us even if not yet in its completed fulness. In the *Large Catechism*, Luther's instruction is clear: we are not left to step into this future alone, nor are we left alone to become the human beings we are yet to be. God is creating and bringing forth in us what we cannot create or bring forth ourselves. Moreover, God is equipping us for this pilgrimage of becoming; and therefore, faith is always a life of responding to God's initiatives towards us. It is a life lived in liminal space, *a life of becoming what we are yet to be and always a living into the vocation that is being brought forth in us.*

6

Led into Liminality with Only Hope and Prayer—The Security of a Beggar

The Security of a Beggar

LIFE IN THE LIMINAL space of leaving a survival mode of existence for life in baptismal vocation is not easy. At times it is difficult and even dangerous. It is a pilgrimage that does not come with guarantees of ease, comfort, or smooth sailing. Nor is it a pilgrimage with a well defined map or GPS system that offers the immediate awareness of knowing where you are located or how far you are from your destination. As much as it is a pilgrimage driven and directed by the light and vision of God's future, it is at the same time a walk into unknowing, uncertainty, and even darkness. It is a step into borderland reality! And because of this, it will always be a pilgrimage where the light of faith and hope are held in tension with the darkness of fear and doubt!

The messages of triumphal religion that tell us fear and doubt will be conquered and overcome with strong faith is nothing more than the illusory thinking of a theology of glory. In contrast, the paradox of the cross is that as much as fear, doubt, and even despair are obstacles that keep us from living into our human vocation, they are at the same time, the very place where God intervenes into our life with holy encounters. No, God does not encounter us with a quick fix that disseminates or alleviates fear.

Part II: Becoming What We Are Yet to Be

Neither does God encounter us as one who gives us the self-help manual on how to conquer and overcome it. Rather, God encounters us as one who in her hiddenness enters and leads us into these dark places of doubt and fear, leading us into the hope filled daylight of a future we cannot see to be sure, yet entering into darkness none the less. This is the story of Jesus' passion and death! We do not follow because we can see clearly see the way, the map, or tangible outcomes of victory that somehow give us immunity to fear's power. We follow in faith, and faith will always have to do with believing, trusting, and following what cannot be seen or validated by the conventional means of gaining security and control so prevalent in our self-absorbed culture. Mary Solberg says it well:

> Articulated in terms of the theology of the cross, faith involves an entrance into darkness: the casting away of all man-made notions of God, even of all man-made initiatives toward God. The cross confounds all human expectations . . . Out of these depths, the human cries for help to the God who cannot be seen. This is the beginning of faith, a forsaking of the illusion that one can save oneself, justify oneself, give oneself life.[1]

Hall describes the pilgrimage of faith this way:

> The true *Christian life* is not a life of *securitas*, lived out in the midst of a world in which the triumph of good is assured. On the contrary, to enter upon such a life is to be denied every form of security. The only real security is the security of the beggar. It entails being stripped of everything (human beings) call security and safety . . .[2]

Solberg and Hall's points are well exemplified by the disciples after Jesus' death. Mark tells us that they are mourning and weeping, apparently not having ventured out of the room where they have been holed up.[3] After all, Jesus, the leader of the movement, has been killed by the political and religious leaders powers that be. Why wouldn't they be next? They have no protection against such powers. Even after Jesus appears and commands them to leave the room and get out into the world, they leave without any security or protection against the powers and threats they will encounter. They venture into unknowing and uncertainty without any immunity to

---

1. Solberg, *Compelling Knowledge*, 91.
2. Hall, *Lighten our Darkness*, 119.
3. Mark 16: 10, NRSV.

vulnerability, fear, or death. What they do have is the promise Jesus gives them in Matthew's telling of the Ascension: "Lo, I am with you to the close of the age"—and that is enough![4]

If entering the pilgrimage of becoming what we are yet to be in these perilous times is entering into a life stripped of everything we consider safety and security as Solberg and Hall describe, then entering into the pilgrimage of leaving survival for vocation means entering into the very same places as the disciples, the risky places of unknowing and uncertainty without any of the securities and safety nets our triumphal religion would tell us we must have. The only security we have is a beggar's security.[5] And that beggar's security is in the God we cannot see, yet the God into whose sustaining mercy we throw ourselves when we forsake the illusion that we can save ourselves or give ourselves life, especially as we leave survival to live in the pilgrimage of becoming a culture of life.

Life Under the Cross—A Community and Communion of Prayer

In his book of daily meditations, *Gift and Task,* Walter Brueggemann shares a conversation he had with Hans Walter Wolff, the noted University of Heidelberg Old Testament theologian. In the 1930s, Wolff had been a young pastor in the Confessing Church of Germany when it resisted Hitler and the National Socialist movement. Years later, Brueggemann asked him what resources the Confessing Church had to sustain its faith and resistance to what was happening. He recalled that without hesitation Wolff responded: "We prayed and sang hymns, and we wrote many letters to each other."[6] Ponder, for a moment, the significance of those words. In the face of the perils and threats of one of the most evil authoritarian regimes in history, this resisting and confessing Christian community found its power to resist and hold forth in prayer, in singing hymns, and in their constant communication with each other through letter writing. In other words, they became

---

4. Mt 28:20, NRSV.

5. The reference to "a beggar's security" is based on words reported to have been Luther's last as he was dying, "We are beggars. That is true." They reflect his faith and theological conviction that human creatures are totally incapable of creating refuge, security, and well being within themselves. Like a beggar, their life is totally dependent on what is given to them by God from outside of their own being. Cf. *LW* 54:476.

6. Brueggemann, *Gift and Task,* 254.

Part II: Becoming What We Are Yet to Be

and lived into being a culture of life in the face of death. What stands out in Wolff's reflection is that in the living out of their discipleship and resistance, the words of their prayers and hymns were yoked with the actions of their letter writing, communication which was surely a mutual sharing of the suffering they were enduring as well as a sharing of the gospel's encouragement and hope.

Of this yoked connection between words and actions, Craig Nessan, of Wartburg Seminary, says:

> When we consider the intercessions that we pray not only in our personal petitions but in our Christian assemblies, we are invited to enter the deep suffering of the world. This includes all those known to us by name who belong to or are connected to a given congregation—the sick, dying, grieving, injured, unemployed, or fearful ones—but for the needs of the world and all of creation. These intercessions are not merely a means to hand over to God things that are too difficult for us. Instead our intercessions are a call to discipleship. If we dare to pray by name for the needs of the sick, grieving, or those in harm's way, the church of Jesus Christ is called to enter and share the burdens of these very people: sending messages of solidarity, visiting them, devising acts of kindness, and exercising agency to mitigate their suffering, whatever that might cost us. The integrity of the church depends on authenticity between what we profess, in this case that for which we pray, and how we embody those words in deeds.[7]

When the community of the Confessing Church came together to pray, they did exactly what Nessan described: they entered the deep suffering of the world; their prayers were a call to be in discipleship even as they were situated in the horrors of war; and they shared the sufferings of one another in spite of what it might have cost.

That's what cultures of life do in the work of resisting the dark powers and threats of death. It's what we do when we leave survival modes of existence for life in our baptismal vocation. As strange as it will sound, the Confessing Church of Germany was not in a survival mode of existence; they were living into their baptismal vocation, in spite of the powers and threats in which they were situated. And in so doing, the faith they professed in Jesus the Christ and the words of their prayers were embodied in the actions of the solidarity they had with each other and with those around

---

7. Nessan, *Free Indeed*, 99.

them who were the victims of Nazi terror. Their yoked connection between words and actions is what gave their community authenticity and integrity.

In contrast, I share another story. On Nov. 9, 2018, the day after her son was killed in a random shooting at a bar in Southern California, Susan Orfanos angrily declared, "I don't want prayers, I don't want thoughts, I want gun control." Through her tears she pleaded for Congress to "pass gun control so no one else has a child that doesn't come home."[8] Given the violence that had just been inflicted on her child and the grief with which she was left to carry, her vehement rage was understandable; yet to many ears, especially Christian ears, her words, might have been offensive. How could anyone refuse the kindness of prayers and thoughts in a time of grief?

Offensive though her words might have sounded, they spoke to a truth our privatized worlds of faith need to hear: when kind thoughts and prayers are extended as a way of offering comfort to victims of the devastations to which we have referred throughout this discussion, yet are not accompanied by tangible acts or a willingness to stand along side them to resist those devastations, the prayers and thoughts we offer ring hollow and empty. Victims of racism are tired of being "held in thoughts and prayers" that are void of any actions or commitments to do anything about resisting or dismantling it. Victims of economic disparity are tired of being in "held in thoughts and prayers" that ask God to be with the poor and needy, yet see no action or change that might evidence they are truly being held in the hearts of rich and privileged. As Nessan suggests, without any action, they are words that reveal the disconnect between what we say we believe and how we embody those beliefs in in the sharing of the sufferings of the world, a disconnect that leaves our witness to the faith appear inauthentic.

Make no mistake. Yoking the words of our faith and prayers with the deeds and actions that come with entering the deep suffering of the world is where we existentially come to know the truths to which Hall and Solberg referred. It is the place where we come to know that the triumph of good is not assured; it is the place where we must forsake the illusion that we can save ourselves or have life within ourselves. It is the place where we cry for help to the God who we cannot see nor even validate, yet the God in whom we can most assuredly trust to give us what we need regardless of the costs we will encounter. It is in this place, along with every other human being who enters this baptismal pilgrimage, that we become a community under the cross and a communion of prayer.

8. *Guardian*, "Mother of California Shooting Victim."

Part II: Becoming What We Are Yet to Be

The Lord's Prayer—Equipped to Become a Culture of Life in the Midst of Death

Let's be honest. The Lord's Prayer is the most familiar and most prayed prayer we know. Hardly a gathering of Christians takes place without it being uttered. Even persons who are not frequent occupiers of church pews on Sunday morning have familiarity with it and will be able to say its words. It is a liturgical ritual that has been embedded into our memories from childhood. Yet, to paraphrase Brueggemann's words, the Lord's Prayer is a prayer widely prayed, but a prayer greatly reduced. It is a prayer that has been flattened, ritualized, trivialized, and rendered inane. Partly, it is simply an old habit among us, neither valued nor questioned.[9]

Consider for a moment the context in which Jesus taught this prayer to his disciples. They simply asked, "Lord, teach us to pray."[10] We might rightfully ask why they needed to be taught to pray in the first place. After all, they weren't novices in the Jewish tradition so we might assume that they already had knowledge and experience with prayer. Yet here they are asking to be taught to pray. Why? Might it be that in asking Jesus to teach them to pray, they were actually asking Jesus *to equip them for the work that was in front of them,* that is to equip them for the vocational work and calling into which they were now living. We might assume that they did in fact have familiarity with prayer. What they didn't know how to do was pray in such a way so as to ask for the equipping they needed to live into the vocation of being citizens of the Kingdom, a way of life they were coming to realize was different from the religious life they had known. Jesus does not hesitate to teach them.

Having said that, we should not think of being equipped in the same way as in our present culture. In this regard, Joseph Sittler observes that equipment refers to "that which we need to do the thing we want or ought or are called to do . . ." In contrast, however, he notes that equipment also means "an internal nurture, an internal formation that matures one's competence for an appointed task."[11] Using Sittler's observation, we might say that the disciples were not asking to be equipped with tools, strategies, and data that would facilitate their work; they were asking for the internal nurture, formation, and maturity into competence for the vocation into which they

---

9. Brueggemann, *Finally Comes the Poet*, 1–2.
10. Mt 6:9–13; Lk 11: 2–4.
11. Sittler, *Gravity and Grace*, 29–30.

were being called. In Luke's rendition of this narrative, that's exactly what Jesus assures the disciples they will be given when they pray and ask for it. Using an image they would know about he tells them: if you know how to give your children gifts, how much more will your heavenly Father give the Holy Spirit to those who ask him.[12] In other words, when asking for God's gifts in this prayer, they can be assured that they will be equipped with the Holy Spirit to engage the work to which they have been called to engage.

Knowing their need to be equipped for what they were stepping into, we can imagine that the disciples' use and praying of this prayer was not flattened, ritualized, or trivialized. It had meaning and purpose because it came from their awareness of what they needed. Perhaps that is why our use and praying of it has become a ritualized, old habit among us that is prayed without much energy or emotion: it is coming from lips and hearts that lack awareness of our need to be equipped for the pilgrimage of stepping into their baptismal vocation. Luther's words in his introduction to the Lord's Prayer speak to this lack of awareness.

> But where there is to be true prayer, there must be utter earnestness. We must feel our need, the distress that drives and impels us to cry out. Then prayer will come spontaneously, as it should, and no one will need to be taught how to prepare for it, or how to create the proper devotion. This need, however, that ought to concern us . . . is something you will find richly in the Lord's Prayer . . . For we are lacking plenty of things: all that is missing is that we do not feel or see them. God therefore wants you to lament and express your needs and concerns, not because God is unaware of them, but in order that you may kindle your heart to stronger and greater desires and open your apron to receive many things.[13]

Standing in the liminal space between what we are and what we are becoming, the beggar's security given in the Lord's Prayer is simply this: in its words and petitions, we are asking that God would nurture, form, and mature us into a competency to become what we are yet to be. In other words, it is a prayer that asks for the Spirit of God to transform us into a culture of life and prevent us from being conformed to the world and its powers that seek to undo life. When prayed from the position of knowing how desperately we want and need God to do this transforming work in us, the Lord's Prayer can no longer be prayed as a flattened and ritualized set of

---

12. Lk 11:1–12, NRSV.
13. *TLC*, 371.

words. Rather it will be prayed from the heart with the assurance that God will respond and give us what we need to live into the transforming work she is doing in us.

Keeping God's Name Holy, Being the Kingdom, Doing God's Will

Living into God's saving and transforming work begins with the mindfulness that God is holy. Once again, that seems like a no-brainer. What Christian doesn't believe that? Yet in a world of many gods and lords that seek our servitude, we are seduced into making many things and people "holy" when they aren't, and in making them "holy," we give our lives to them. Our ability to discern what is holy from what is not is greatly diminished in a culture of self-absorbed narcissism. If something serves our own purposes and self-fulfillment, we call it good and holy, even thinking that "God has blessed us real good." When asked why we pray for God's name to be holy when it is already holy, Luther's answer was: "Yes, in its essence it is already holy, but our use of it is not holy."[14] We cannot step into God's transforming work without this mindfulness. Without it, living into the kingdom of God and the culture of life is obstructed. Discerning and doing God's will are likewise hindered, although we might live in the illusion that we are participants in the kingdom and doing God's will when in fact we aren't.

So what does it mean to keep God's name holy? Luther answers this with an explanation of its opposite, what it means to profane God's name.

> Now the name of God is profaned by us in either word or deeds . . . In the first place, then, it is profaned when people, preach, teach, and speak in the name of God anything that is false and deceptive, using God's name to dress up their lies and make them acceptable; this is the worst desecration and dishonor of the divine name. Likewise when people grossly misuse the divine name as a cover for their shame, by swearing, conjuring, etc. In the next place, it is profaned by an openly evil life and wicked works, when those who are called Christians and God's people are adulterers, drunkards, gluttons, jealous persons and slanderers. Here again God's name is necessarily being profaned and blasphemed because of us.[15]

If the truth be told, it doesn't take long to see how in a culture of self-absorbed narcissism it is easy to fall into the behaviors Luther described,

14. *TLC*, 372.
15. *TLC*, 373–74.

Led into Liminality with Only Hope and Prayer—The Security of a Beggar

even without our knowing it. More to the point, it is easy to fall into the trap of profaning God's name with the illusion that we are keeping it holy. Like an addict who lives in the denial of his addiction, it is to be seduced by the gods and lords of this world into believing that the pursuit of pleasure, wealth, and power is what God wants for us—as attested to by so many of our culture's mega churches and popular televangelism. And that is why this petition becomes so vital if we are to live into what we are becoming. We desperately need the mindfulness and courage to "call a thing what it is" when we are being detracted by the gods and lords of this world—in our private lives, our communal lives, and yes even in our congregations.

For Luther, God's name is kept holy when it is given honor and praise This honor and praise is not just in our words and speech, but in our outward actions and deeds directed towards our neighbor in need. We are reminded of something said in our discussion on the creed: God is praised when creation and human community work as they are intended. Keeping God's name holy in this manner takes us to what we ask of God in the second and third petitions, let your kingdom come and your will be done on earth as in heaven. The story of Susan Orfanos and her rage at hollow thoughts and prayers that are void of any willingness to connect words with deeds and actions remind us of why we pray these petitions. We need boldness and courage to step out of our passive silence so that our thoughts and words are yoked with actions, regardless of what those actions might cost. It is a boldness and courage we cannot muster on our own.

The story of what happened to Jesus' disciples during his passion is a helpful illustration of why these two petitions are so vitally important to the pilgrimage of leaving survival for vocation. The fact is, for all of their bravado about staying faithful to Jesus even unto death, they ran away and deserted him when they realized what the rulers and powers that be were going to do to him. In the face of death, their words of allegiance proved to be hollow and empty.

Yes, their desertion is not the full story, for we know what happens after Jesus' resurrection and ascension. Nevertheless, what they did in the immediate moment of being confronted with the dreadful enormity of the powers that be and what they will do when their power is challenged should tell us something about ourselves. When challenged, the power and backlash of these powers are enormous and they can overwhelm us into retreat and silence. Luther well understood this when he wrote,

Part II: Becoming What We Are Yet to Be

> . . . like a furious foe, the devil raves and rages with all its power and might, marshaling all is subjects and even enlisting the world and our own flesh as its allies. For our flesh is in itself vile and inclined to evil, even when we have accepted God's word and believe it . . . .the devil stirs things up, feeding and fanning the flames, in order to impede us, put us to flight, cut us down, and bring us once again under its power.[16]

In the face of the backlashes that come when we want to stand in solidarity with the victims of racism, hate, gun violence, environmental and economic injustice, we know our tendency. Like the disciples, we are tempted to run and hide, and often we do. Like them, we lose our heart! And that is exactly why we pray these words, let your kingdom come and let your will be done. For in the words of these petitions, we are asking God for nothing less than to equip our hearts with the trust, resilience, and courage to stand forth when the powers of racial hate and injustice, violence, and greed are in our face and threatening our very lives. In these petitions, we are asking God to equip us in such a way that we not lose heart and desert Jesus when we are called upon to take risks for the good of our neighbor. We are asking that in these moments, God empower us to *be the kingdom, not just represent it!* For as Luther reminds us, the kingdom is not afar off. It is in us.[17]

Give us What We Need—A Prayer for Ourselves and the World

At the center of Luther's instruction on the fourth petition, "Give us our daily bread," stands this fundamental belief already asserted in his explanations to the first commandment and the first article of the creed: God wants life for every human being on the planet, which means that as creator of all that exists, he brought creation into being with the intent that it would provide for every human being's nourishment and sustenance. No exceptions. Moreover, the purpose of human community—including all of its civil, political affairs and its means for organizing itself—is to ensure that all have access to creation's provisions, not just a few.

At the beginning of his instruction on this the petition, Luther writes:

> Now, our life requires not only food and clothing and other necessities for our body, but also peace and concord in our daily

16. *TLC*, 377.
17. *LW* 42:41.

activities, associations, and situations of every sort with the people among whom we live and with whom interact—in short, in everything that pertains to the regulation of both our domestic and our civil or political affairs. For where those two spheres are interfered with and prevented from functioning as they should, there the necessities of life are also interfered with and life cannot be maintained for any length of time.[18]

In the last words of that sentence, "life cannot be maintained for any length of time," he was not referring just to the life of the disenfranchised who live on the margins of life; he was referring to all of life, including all of us who live in privileged affluence. In this short sentence, Luther makes clear that we are a human community; when the necessities of life are threatened and interfered with, our life as a human community cannot be maintained for very long.

We are keenly aware of how our self-absorbed narcissism has caused us to lose sight of creation's interdependency. It has caused us to go awry in our culture's attitude that creation is here to serve our self-indulgent appetites, the attitude that we can have what we want when we want it regardless of who may pay the price; it has caused us to believe that we rightfully deserve to have what we want because we can afford it. It has caused us to be more concerned and faithful to our political ideologies and desires for power than to the common good and welfare of all. It has caused us to forget that we are but part of the whole human community, not gods unto ourselves. To use Luther's words, it is our narcissism that has interfered with the two spheres, civil and political, which means that the necessities of life have been interfered with and life cannot be maintained for any length of time.

Luther's insight intersects with every issue we have named in this discussion. The basic necessities of life, including the peace, concord, and tranquility that make a productive life possible, are interfered with when racism stands in the way of fair and equitable employment. The necessities of life are interfered with when gun violence prevents children to attend school without living with the constant fear and anxiety of being shot. The necessities of life are interfered with when the widening gap between the rich and the poor prevents many in this world from having the nutrition they need for life. The necessities of life are diminished if not obliterated altogether when forests are eliminated to grow and feed more cattle to satisfy

---

18. *TLC*, 379.

our appetites for red meat. They are increasingly diminished by pollution that creates toxic water. The list could go on.

Out of his personal experience and his medieval mindset, Luther understood all of these interferences to be the work of evil, or to use his word, the devil. But he also understood that in asking God for daily bread and all of the necessities of life, we are also asking God to mitigate against interference and every work prevents human beings from having and rightly enjoying these necessities. He comments, "When you say and ask for "daily bread," you ask for everything that is necessary in order to have and enjoy daily bread and, on the contrary, against everything that interferes with enjoying it."[19] Later in his explanation he stated more directly,

> . . . especially is this petition directed against our chief enemy, the devil, whose whole purpose and desire is to take away or interfere with all we have received from God . . . The devil is not satisfied to obstruct and overthrow the spiritual order by deceiving souls with its lies and bringing them under its power, but it also prevents and impedes the establishment of any kind of government or honorable and peaceful relations on earth. In short, it pains the devil that anyone should receive even a mouthful of bread from God and eat it in peace.[20]

Whether we take Luther's use of the word, devil, literally or not, the clear and strong implication of his assertion is that all of our narcissistic behaviors make us participants in evil's work of interfering with the gifts we have received from God. If as Luther suggests, that in asking God to give us the necessities required for our nourishment and sustenance we are at the same time asking God to work against everything that interferes with her provision, then I suggest that his instruction also means we are asking God to equip us so as to restrain our own narcissistic behaviors and actions that deprive others from having what they need. If the Lord's Prayer is a prayer asking God to do her transforming work in us so that we might be a transforming culture of life in the world, then this petition is our request that she not only provide us with the basic necessities of life, but that she also grant us the agency and courage to stand against anything that is depriving our neighbor of life, including our own actions and behaviors—even the passive behavior of keeping silent while our neighbor cries out in need. Yes, this includes racism, gun violence, exploitation in all of its

19. *TLC*, 379.
20. *TLC*, 381.

form, environmental injustice and abuse of the earth, power domination, economic disparity between the rich and the poor, and the list goes on. To pray for such agency and courage is to ask God to give us what we need to embody the culture of life authentically and with integrity by stepping into the deep sufferings of the world to help those who are the victims of death's powers have what they need for life.

Equipped to Offer Grace—Forgiven as We Forgive Others

It goes without saying that we live in a deeply divisive time. There is seemingly no issue that we can put on the table without being divided between left and right, blue and red, conservative and liberal. The divisions are no longer on the surface. They run deep, dividing not only a nation, but communities, neighborhoods, families—and even religious communities and Christian congregations. These divisions have evolved into an even deeper schism that is characterized by the vehemence and hostility emerging between the extremes of each side of the divisions, a vehemence which has caused us to see those who are on "the other side" as the enemy. We seem to have lost our capacity to forgive, seek healing, and restore relationships. Instead we opt to blame each other for our adversities and problems. Increasingly, we rely on retaliation and revenge as a way of getting justice or at least getting satisfaction for the ills and harms we think have been inflicted on us by the beliefs or actions of others. One way or the other, we seem to be caught in an ever tightening knot that is becoming so tight it cannot be loosed or untied without significant consequences.

In the midst of these dangerous and life threatening divisions, Christians gather every Sunday morning and ask God to "forgive our sins as we forgive those who sin against us." This petition, along with the third article of the creed in which we claim to believe in forgiveness as a way of life, expresses the foundational reality and paradox of forgiving our enemies, a reality and paradox into which Christians are called to live and practice. We are literally called upon to forgive those who have inflicted a wrong or an injury upon us. What can be more difficult to do when the flames of anger and vengeance spew within us, crying out for pay back, revenge, and retaliation? Yet here is Jesus who in his dying asks God to forgive those who have inflicted upon him the most brutal and shameful punishment known in the Roman world.

Is it any wonder that Jesus included this petition in the prayer he taught his disciples? He knew the struggles we would have living and practicing the work of forgiveness in a world that lives by vengeance and retaliation. Like the rest of the Lord's Prayer, its intent is to ask God to equip with us with the courage to defy our desires for vengeance and retaliation so as to offer forgiveness to our neighbor, yes even our enemies and those who have wronged us. Nowhere is this courage to love enemies and those who have inflicted a harm more profoundly expressed than in Jesus' words from the cross as he was dying from the brutalities inflicted by his enemies: "Father forgive them for they do not know what they are doing."[21]

Luther was keenly aware that forgiving one's enemies and those who have committed a wrong was intrinsically and inextricably linked to receiving God's forgiveness. One does not come without the other.

> God has promised us assurance that everything is forgiven and pardoned yet on the condition that we also forgive our neighbor. For just as we sin greatly against God every day and yet God forgives it all through grace, so we must also forgive our neighbor who does us harm, violence, and injustice, bears malice toward us, etc. If you do not forgive, do not think that God forgives you. But if you forgive, you have the comfort and assurance that you are forgiven in heaven—not on account of your forgiving . . . but instead because God has set this up for our strengthening and assurance as a sign along with the promise that matches this petition in Luke 6:37, "Forgive, and you will be forgiven."[22]

On the surface, this sounds like a *quid pro quo*. It is not. Rather, it is about the spirit and atmosphere that results when forgiveness is not kept a private matter between the individual and God without any impact on relationships with neighbors, but instead becomes an intentional action and spirit emanating from a forgiven and liberated heart. It is the same spirit of grace with which God extends God's forgiveness towards us. It is a power that breaks down the toxic air and spirit of blame and vengeance. Of forgiveness' power, Stjerna says,

> Forgiveness is the heart matter of justification and reconciled relatonship with God and also the most powerful force in human interactions . . . justification is lived out in the tension between

---

21. Lk 23:34, NRSV.
22. *TLC*, 383.

being liberated by a word of forgiveness oneself while out of that liberation granting forgiveness for others from what binds them.[23]

Stjerna's assertion that forgiveness is the most powerful force in human interactions is given testimony in the work and witness of Martin Luther King Jr. and his leadership in the civil rights movement. In a blog appearing on Seton Hall University's website, *Love and Forgiveness in Governance,* Ernest Ogbozor reflects on the power of love and forgiveness in King's work and leadership.

> Despite MLK's several arrests and detentions, he drew strength from the power of love, forgiveness and non-violence. MLK said: "Forgiveness does not mean ignoring what has been done or putting a false label on an evil act." It means, rather, that the evil act no longer remains as a barrier to the relationship. He further said that forgiveness is a catalyst creating the atmosphere necessary for a fresh start and a new beginning, and we are free from the mental block that impede new relationships. Forgiveness means reconciliation, a coming together again. Without this, no man can love his enemies. The degree to which we are able to forgive determines the degree to which we are able to love our enemies.[24]

King's belief that forgiveness is the catalyst that changes a toxic atmosphere to life giving air and removes the obstacles that prevent healing and relational restoration is of paramount importance to our discussion. This is exactly what living into the transformative power of a culture of life means. If it is a culture that truly lives, practice, and embodies the way of forgiveness, then it will be the most powerful force in human interactions as Stjerna describes.

If forgiveness is the catalyst that transforms a toxic atmosphere into one that is life giving, then we can no longer think of it merely as words spoken that will somehow or magically bring immediate healing and resolution to a conflict without the intentional and hard work that must follow. To use Nessan's words, if forgiveness is to have integrity and authenticity, the words that are spoken must be yoked with action and deeds that will embody a new tone, spirit, and atmosphere in which the broken relationship has existed. In a culture of affluence that likes to live in pretense, illusion, and play nice, it is easy to project the persona that we have forgiven someone or some group, yet in our spirit hold on to the grudges, hostilities,

---

23. *TLC,* 383.
24. Ogbozor, "Martin Luther King, Jr. lines 50–58.

and animosities that have been there all along. It is easy to play nice without changing anything. We forget that regardless of the persona we are trying to project, what is in our spirit will eventually make its way into what we embody forth. Forgiveness, whether it is being received or given is always a matter of the heart that extends to bodily action. One only need to look at how this gets lived out in congregations involved in conflicts. We share the peace, a visible symbol of living in the spirit and atmosphere of forgiveness and reconciliation, yet when we depart the toxic atmosphere of animosity and hostility remains in our hearts, underground though it may be.

Our culture's propensity to believe that forgiveness means we are to forget, gloss over, or minimize whatever wrong or harm has been inflicted is a grave mistake. For King, forgiveness means no such thing. Forgiveness means that we change the tone, spirit, and atmosphere in which we address and engage those wrongs and harms that have been inflicted on us or that we have inflicted on others. Forgiveness means we do not address those wrongs and harms with a spirit of vengeance or a spirit of self-justification whereby we strive to gain dominance over the other by proving them wrong and ourselves right. As Luther reminded us, forgiveness means engaging the wrongs and harms we have inflicted on each other in the same way God has addressed the wrongs and harms we have committed against her—in a spirit of grace. And God's grace towards us is never intended to be a cover up, a minimizing, nor a gloss over our wrongs. It is the certainty that we are never cut off from God because of what we have done, but are continually brought into the transforming power of God's love so as to change. It is in the spirit and atmosphere of God's grace that we are to "call a thing what it is," and not run away from it.

Having said that, we cannot ignore the fact that key to "calling a thing what it is" and not running away from it is to know within our hearts the contrition, repentance and remorse that comes when we realize the truths of the wrongs and harms we have inflicted on others. It is then to take the next step of being able to say with integrity and authenticity, "I am truly sorry for what I have done." It is to say these words with an earnest and heart felt desire to change our attitudes and actions towards the person or persons on whom our wrongs have been inflicted. At the same time, if we are to live in the spirit and atmosphere of forgiveness we say we believe in, then this work of forgiveness is not just to offer our contrition to those we have wronged, it is to receive their contrition when they offer it to us and ask for our forgiveness. It matters not whether we are the ones asking

Led into Liminality with Only Hope and Prayer—The Security of a Beggar

for forgiveness or the ones being asked to forgive, forgiveness is always a matter of living into the change and the new ways of living and being in relationship that it makes possible.

It doesn't take long to see just how difficult this work really is in a self-absorbed culture that teaches us the art and craft of pretentious self-righteousness, an art and craft that does not allow for the humility or the courage to take the risk of saying, "I was wrong, and I am truly sorry for what I have done to you." Likewise, it is a culture that does not teach us how to receive the contrition of others with humility and grace so as to put away our pride and say with authenticity and integrity, "I forgive you." It is a culture that teaches us blame, retribution, revenge and power domination are the best ways to find satisfaction, not forgiveness—yes even in Christian congregations.

When we think of forgiveness in this way, we can see just how much our vitriolic and divided culture needs the church. No, it does not need a church that proclaims self-righteous words of forgiveness and love, yet whose actions and ways of being a community are not yoked with those words. It needs a church who in its way of being a community of forgiveness actually practices that forgiveness in its life together, especially when it is in conflict and division.

But this is not the only witness the church has to offer when it comes to the practice of forgiveness. It will bear witness to the power of forgiving and being forgiven by its capacity to provide the very atmosphere in which risky and dangerous conversations can take place, an atmosphere where we are able to take the risk of being encountered by the prophetic voices of our time that are calling us to accountability for the wrongs we have committed against each other. These are the voices that are calling us to accountability for our passive silence and complicity in the powers of racism, environmental injustice and abuse, gun violence, economic disparity, and the list goes on. It is an atmosphere where these prophetic voices do not speak out of a need for pay back or retaliation, but are voices that are calling us into the hard and difficult work of healing and reconciliation. As we referenced earlier, these risky conversations must be carried out in an atmosphere where we can hear the suffering and harms of the victims on whom those sufferings have been inflicted—from their point of view and experience, not our own! Moreover, we need to hear the extent to which our passivity and silence has made us a complicit participant in the infliction of the ills they have suffered. This is the atmosphere of contrition, being forgiven, and forgiving—the atmosphere and spirit of grace—into which the gospel is calling us to live. It is the atmosphere that opens up new beginnings and new ways of living with each other in true and authentic community.

The world and our culture do not need a church of words. It needs a church—a culture of life—whose words of love and forgiveness will be yoked with deeds and actions that will give those words integrity and authenticity. Trusting in the power of forgiveness, whether given or received, the church—the culture of life—will have the capacity to change the vitriolic climate of hate and division to a life giving atmosphere of peace and concord. To be sure, it sounds idealistic and naive. Yet this is exactly what we say the church is when we confess in the creed, "I believe in the holy catholic church, the communion of saints, and the forgiveness of sins . . ." In this petition, that is exactly what we are asking God to equip us to become.

Deliverance From Temptation and Evil

In spite of the parental tone with which Luther often writes, the power of his theology is in the fact that he was a scholar and theologian with a pastoral and empathic heart. Everything he wrote or preached was for the strengthening of the human heart and soul, for the sustenance of faith in the face of the powers of evil and death—and the Small and Large Catechisms are no exception. His passion was more than just that he wanted people to have faith, he was passionate that the integrity and authenticity of that faith be evidenced in the extent to which their words of faith were yoked with actions and deeds. Yet, he knew all too well from his own life experience as well as the human experiences he encountered in his pastoral care of others, the extent to which baptized Christians, no matter how strong their faith, are vulnerable and susceptible to evil's power that seduces and detracts them from their vocational calling. If truth be told, we know how true this is in our own culture and time. As much as conventional religion in our self-absorbed culture tells us that we have within us the capacity to overcome and deliver ourselves from these demonic and life threatening powers, we know we do not. We know the extent to which we are vulnerable to stumbling and collapsing into evil's grasp, even when our intentions are otherwise. And that is precisely why in these last two petitions, "lead us not into temptation and deliver us from evil," we ask God to equip us with the strength to withstand and resist these powers when they come upon us. At the very beginning of his explanation to the sixth petition, Luther says:

> We have now heard enough about the trouble and effort it takes to retain and persevere in all the gifts for which we pray. This, however, is not accomplished without failures and stumbling. Moreover, although we have acquired forgiveness and a good conscience and have been wholly absolved, yet such is life that one stands today and falls tomorrow. Therefore, even though at present we are upright and stand before God with a good conscience, we must ask once again that God will not allow us to fall and collapse under attacks and temptations.[25]

In our self-absorbed culture it is easy—and convenient—to hear the words of these two petitions as references to the temptations and evils that encounter us in our privatized worlds. But as we have seen throughout this discussion, Luther's instruction compels us to look beyond our privatized faith to ask how these petitions pertain to our culture of self-indulgence and self-preservation. And what do these petitions mean in a culture that purports belief and trust in God and yet has fallen prey to the powers of violence, greed, pride, envy all of which have resulted in the devastations of dehumanization, exploitation, and power domination in its many forms? Indeed, these petitions do pertain to the individual and private struggles all of us have in living and being faithful to what we say we believe. However, in a culture stuck in survival modes of living that are inflicting harms on neighbors and the earth, it is necessary and even urgent that we pay attention to what we are really asking of God when we pray these petitions.

As we have noted throughout this discussion, ours is a culture of illusion. As religious as it purports to be—and on the surface it would appear to be just that—its guiding theology is a theology of glory. Recalling Luther's distinction between a theology of glory and a theology of the cross, we are reminded that it is a theology of illusion and pretense. It is a theology that looks for and validates God in the illusions and pretenses of wealth, power, successes, and triumph. Unlike a theology of the cross, it cannot fathom the God who is hidden in the depths of our humanness, in the depths of our sufferings and dyings. And unlike a theology of the cross, a theology of glory cannot imagine a God who leads us into darkness as a way of leading us into her future, nor can it imagine a God who leads us into these journeys without any security but the security of a beggar. Our senses have been so distorted by affluence and self-absorption that they can neither imagine or perceive such a God. That is why it is critical to ask God to equip us with

---

25. *TLC*, 384.

the capacity to trust and believe in what we cannot see in such a way that we are able to resist the powerful temptations that challenge and confront us.

As Luther suggested, even for a person of strong faith, living in this culture of illusion comes with the intense temptation to live in its pretentious way of life; it also comes with the reality of our vulnerability to evil's demonic grasp on our life. No doubt there are many temptations, personal and cultural, that we might identify and that could be named as we pray these petitions. I suggest, however, that living within this self centered culture as we do, there are two that ought be in the forefront of asking God to equip us to resist the temptations this culture daily throws our way: the temptation of denial and the temptation of believing and placing our trust in false security.

The Temptation of Denial

The temptation of denial is not so much the temptation to deny God's existence, although that is always a prevailing inclination, especially when in the throes of suffering or feeling abandoned by God. The denial to which we refer is the denial that comes when we live in the illusion that nothing is wrong with us when in fact it is. Denial is the refusal to "call a thing what it is"; it is to minimize the devastations in which we live, and to minimize the harms we are inflicting on others through our ways of living. In this regard, we have succumbed to denial and are held in its grasp when as affluent white people we refuse to acknowledge our racism, and the extent to we are participating in racist behaviors when we remain silent and refuse even to have conversations about it. It is the same denial and minimization that takes place in our refusal to acknowledge the realities of global warming and environmental abuse; and our refusal to change and adapt the behaviors contributing to earth's demise is even a greater denial. It is the same denial taking place when we hear the cries of those who are the victims of gun violence and domestic terrorism. Our inclination to stay silent or refuse to advocate for stricter gun laws as if it makes no difference to us one way or another if those laws are not implemented is yet another form of minimization and denial.

I share a part of my personal history as an illustration. I am a diabetic as is just about every other male in my family. Fortunately, I am able to keep it under control with diet, moderate exercise, medication and regular check ups with my physician. Having said that, however, I am always tempted to believe, in fact more times than not, that it is not as serious as it can be. I try maintain a healthy diet, but I can be pretty lax about what or how much I put into my body when there is good food and libation in front of me. While my health is a concern, what is immediately in front of me at the moment becomes more important. Diabetes is one of those diseases, at least in its early stages or if kept under control, can be like an underground infestation. You might have a symptom or two, but nothing worrisome. On the whole you feel good, you don't see any immediate or adverse effects, so you are tempted to live without any mindfulness that you have a potentially serious disease. What you begin to forget is that diabetes is not isolated from the rest of your body's systemic functioning. Almost automatically, a diabetic is vulnerable to having related issues with blood pressure, cholesterol, heart disease, kidney disease, and even blindness. For a diabetic living in the minimization of their disease and the dangers and risks it poses to their body, diabetes will eventually have its demonic and deathly grasp on their entire body, and death will be closer than they thought or wanted if they do not keep it managed and restrained.

That is the power of denial, and that is exactly the same power it has in our narcissistic and self-absorbed culture. It prevents us from seeing and believing how interconnected and interdependent we are as a human community. It prevents us from seeing how our self-indulgent actions will have a systemic impact on others. It narrows our focus to indulging in the pleasures and ways of life that are immediately in front of us, encouraging us to participate in them without regard for how that indulgence will impact the systemic functioning of the rest of society, our community, or even the world. It is what Luther called the temptation of the "flesh."

> ... it goes to work and lures us daily into unchaste, laziness, gluttony and drunkenness, greed and deceit, into acts of fraud and deception against our neighbor—in short, into all kinds of evil lusts that by nature cling to us and to which we are incited by association and example of other peopled by things we hear and see. All this often wounds and inflames even an innocent heart.[26]

---

26. *TLC*, 384.

Part II: Becoming What We Are Yet to Be

The Temptation to Trust in False Security

In some ways, the temptation to believe and trust in false security is part and parcel of the temptation of denial, yet it merits its own exploration. Like the diabetic who relies on the false security he gets from believing his health is okay, yet is blind to the disease's potential destruction to the whole of his body, our reliance on the false security we get from self-indulged ways of living blind us to the impacts these ways of living have on the rest of the human community. Believing and trusting in false security comes in many forms, and we have alluded to them throughout this discussion, our culture's reliance on wealth, power, status, appearance, and privilege, all of which we look to for refuge, security and well being. As we have seen, our reliance on them blinds us to our greed, envy, pride, and lust, all of which inflict demonic devastations and harms on our neighbors, the human community, and the earth.

There is within our culture and national life, however, another manifestation of reliance on false security to which these petitions call our attention. It is the air of self-righteousness that emerges when we believe we have attained a special status with God because we are Christian. Simply put, self-righteousness is believing with certainty that we are morally superior to everyone else by virtue of our faith. It is the arrogant air we exude in words and actions through which we justify and praise ourselves while at the same time inflict judgment on those we deem less deserving or at worst, less than human.

One of the phrases giving expression to our cultural and national self-righteousness is found in the words, "God bless America." One can hardly drive on a street or highway without seeing a car bearing the bumper sticker, "God Bless America." In similar fashion, it is not uncommon for the song titled with those same words to be sung at sporting and other events, sometimes introduced with the words, "To honor America.." For several decades now, it is almost a ritualized tradition that presidential addresses end with the words, "And may God Bless America." Such adulation has even made its way into Christian worship services. I once attended a worship service where after Holy Communion had been celebrated and the Benediction pronounced, the pastor asked everyone to stand and sing, "God Bless America." The singing of that hymn was accompanied by visual images of the American flag waving across the power point screen, situated in front of the congregation and adjacent to the altar with no awareness or consciousness of how contradictory that image was.

To be sure, in and of themselves, there is nothing wrong with the words, "God Bless America," and there is nothing wrong with feeling the patriotism they inspire. We might even say that if these words were an earnest and heart felt prayer that God bless our country with the courage and wisdom to look with repentant hearts at the harms and injuries it has inflicted on others, then we might agree that they are words worthy of being spoken and prayed. Except we know that's not their purpose or intent. These words are used to express the belief that we are a country who holds special favor with God. Still more pernicious is that we use those words to confirm our self-righteous conviction of being a morally superior culture and nation over every other culture and nation in the world. To ask God to bless America is in reality a prayer asking God to keep us in this place of privilege and superiority even though it is a place that disenfranchises many.

The self-righteousness emerging from trust and belief in false security has another manifestation. It is the belief that special status with God, along with that status' moral superiority, gives us the right and privilege to impose our beliefs and wills on others. It is this self-righteous superiority that gave rise to the white colonization of Africa and other regions of the world. It is the same self-righteous superiority that gave rise to the white man's removal of Native Americans from their tribal lands. It is the same self-righteous superiority that deemed slaves less than human and imbued whites with the demonic belief they had the right to impound blacks as their slaves.

I suggest that this same self-righteousness is now at work in those who believe it their right, an even obligation, to establish a white national Christian movement. Michelle Boorstein, columnist for the Washington Post writes that recent research on this movement suggests that what ties many people and groups together in this movement, "is a shared worldview that Christianity should be fused with civic life and that true Americans are White, culturally conservative and natural born citizens."[27] For proponents of this movement, the fusion of their faith with civic life means the establishment of an authoritarianism that will impose their morality and nationalistic views onto society and the nation. It is a belief that their moral superiority gives the right to make judgment on the behaviors and actions of others. No where is this more evident than in those places where the powers that be, mostly white males, have determined that women who have abortions and the doctors who provide them have committed the criminal act of murder, even when those abortions are medical interventions to save a

---

27. Boorstein, "Christian Nationalists." lines 47–50.

mother's life. This is not intended to be a pro-choice or pro-life statement. Rather it is to show the demonic, incompatible and inharmonious hypocrisy into which self-righteousness leads us. And what can be more incompatible, inharmonious, and demonic than to call these people murderers, while at the same time refusing to enact laws to inhibit and stop gun violence. As Jesus said, "You hypocrite, first take the log out of your own eye, and then you will see clearly to take the speck out of your neighbor's eye."[28]

You get the point. The private and communal temptations with which our culture of affluence and entitlement heap on us are not just temptations into missteps or misdirected deeds. They are temptations into a world of self-righteousness the consequences of which can be dangerous and deadly, especially when that self-righteousness blinds us to our own deeds and actions that inflict harms on others. When blinded to our own sins, we are as vulnerable as we can be to evil's demonic grasp. And so within our culture of narcissistic affluence it is with urgency that we should pray with an earnest heart, "lead us not into temptation, but deliver us from evil."

Amen, Amen, and Amen

For Luther, the "Amen" may well the most important part of prayer, whether that prayer is the Lord's Prayer or any other prayer with which we call upon God's Name, regardless of that prayer's purpose. In Hebrew, it is a word that expresses strong affirmation of something. In his *Exposition on the Lord's Prayer*, he says of the word, Amen, "In German, it means that something is most certainly true. It is good to remember that this word expresses the faith that we should have in praying every petition."[29] For Luther, this is the heart of its importance for prayer. The efficacy of prayer has a great deal to do with the confidence, trust, and certainty with which it is offered, a confidence, trust and certainty that the prayer will be heard and responded to—*even when that confidence, trust, and certainty is faint and dim.* For Luther, Amen is not an end to the prayer. It is actually the beginning, for it gives voice to the belief that what is being prayed for will be granted, even if not the way the pray-or expects. Prayer is not a matter of luck, nor even a matter of *quid pro quo*. Neither is it mechanistic, matter of fact, or mere words. It is always a matter of relational trust.

28. Mt 7:5, NRSV.
29. *LW* 42:76.

> This word (Amen) is nothing else than an unquestioning word of faith on the part of the one who does not pray as a matter of luck but knows that God does not lie because God has promised to grant it. Where there is no faith like this, there can be no true prayer.[30]

As we pray the petitions of the Lord's Prayer, whether in our own words and versions, or in the words we have learned from childhood, we are praying for nothing less than that God will equip us with the gifts and graces to be the kingdom of God in the world, not just people who talk about it. In the words of our discussion we pray that God will equip us to be a culture of life in the face of death's powers. The petitions of the Lord's Prayer are our prayer that God will equip us to stay directed and focused towards God's future of justice, peace, equity, and righteousness for ourselves and for all of creation in spite of all its temptations, evils and threats that will come upon us. And to God we pray and ask these petitions with confidence, Amen! Amen! and Amen!

---

30. *TLC*, 387.

7

Nourished into New Imagination

The Contradiction of Faith—Imagining Beyond Our Senses

THE BAPTISMAL PILGRIMAGE OF leaving survival for vocation is a pilgrimage into God's future. In this pilgrimage we live in and towards that future as if it were now. It is a future to which we direct our lives. Yet, in the face of the perils and threats that surround us, sustaining an empowering confidence and hope in that future is difficult. More to the point, the threats and perils in which we are presently situated diminish our ability to imagine any future beyond our present moment. The realities of death's power are fierce and in our face, and as we have seen, the powers of our culture to tempt us into denial and trust in false securities are enormous. Not long ago, this point was well articulated in a study group that I facilitated. In one particular session, our discussion focused on this very topic of living in and towards future hope. One of the group's participants is an ordained Lutheran deaconess whose background is in environmental engineering. Her present ministry focuses on helping congregations engage issues of global warming and environmental injustice. Towards the end of the conversation, she made this comment: "It's really hard to talk about a future hope or even envision it. I've seen the data, and that data tells us we are toast!" She went on to describe some of the reliable scientific data regarding global warming that validates her claim. But then she went on, "Yet our hope is in a God who does the impossible." Her words could not more aptly describe the reality and the profound contradictions in which we are situated: we place our faith and trust in a God whose future is beyond our comprehension. On the one hand we are situated in an environment that by all accounts is headed towards destruction and the end of life. The political, social, and economic realities do not offer much hope either. Yet, amid all of the data that tells us "we are toast," we have the audacity to believe in and direct our lives towards a creating God and the future into which she is leading us. It is a contradiction to be sure. But that's what imagination of faith does: it invites us to live in the contradictions between the immediacy of what we see in front of us and God's future that is coming at us.

Recently, this astute woman's insight about the difficulty of envisioning a future hope in the face of death took on personal meaning. As the last chapters of this book were being written, a small wildfire broke out in northeastern New Mexico, near where the Sangre De Cristo Mountains meet the prairie grasslands. Over a period of two and a half months, the fire grew to catastrophic proportions, enveloping over three hundred and forty one thousand acres of forest, ranch, and farm land, destroying persons' homes and livelihoods, not to mention its devastating destruction of nature and the area's mountain beauty. As it turned out, the fire destroyed an area where my family has spent considerable time over the past twenty years. It is an area of magnificent splendor and a place that has given our family life giving rest. It is a place that has connected us to God's grace and beauty. Now, it is a very different place. It has become like burnt toast! We find ourselves walking through a forest whose beautiful deep greens have turned to burned blacks and browns. What once were tall stately pines are now nothing but standing black skeletons and tooth picks. Rocks that once displayed brilliant colors in the sunlight are now nothing but charred black; in many places where the burn was severe, the ground is grassless and barren, baked by the fire's intense heat. More devastating are the homes that within minutes were literally reduced to nothing but heaps of ash. Just as disastrous are the water supplies that have become unusable because of the toxins that have drained into watersheds. Seeing, smelling, and feeling all of this devastation, reality set in, a reality for which no optimism or wishful thinking can change: what was will no longer be.

To be sure and as with most fires, new life will eventually emerge in some form. Green will replace the deathly blacks and browns, although the tall trees will be no more, and if they are to return it will not be in my life time. Even with the knowledge that some form of new life and growth will emerge, it is still difficult to imagine or even be hopeful about what that new vegetation and life will look like given that it seems so far off in the future. For now, all we can see, feel, and experience is what is in front of us, death's blacks, browns, and gritty, dirty ashes. Imagining anything beyond this is difficult.

This may seem a strange connection, but somewhere in my reflection on the reality of these devastations, I realized that it was similar and parallel to what I see and experience every day when I hear or read the news and am confronted with the reality of evil and death's power, and what they are doing to our human community and life on this planet. I see death, devastation and not much evidence of anything life giving. Like trying to imagine what a renewed and revitalized forest will look like when all you see is death, it is difficult to envision a future of justice, equity, peace, mercy, and truth when all you hear or see are the voices and powers of dehumanizing hate, deceitful lies, exploitation, and power domination. When surrounded by these voices and powers, God's future seems far off and distant, at times out of sight.

Some will perhaps read and critique this brief story and reflection as a despairing, hopeless, and sad sack tale. And that it may well be. However, I prefer to think of it in the way Javier Alanís spoke of borderland reality. It is standing in the very place where the existential tensions between hope and hopelessness are real. It is standing on the threshold of new encounters, new awarenesses, and new visions. Walking and viscerally experiencing death's powerful grip on the forest's life and on our life as a human community is the very place where we are confronted and challenged with a crisis of faith. Not unlike in borderland reality, that crisis is the very real and existential moment where faith, trust and confidence in God's bare goodness and future collide with the voices and powers of death that try to make us despair of life, give up, and walk away. It is the very existential moment where trust and confidence in God's bare goodness and future collide with the voices and powers of death that tempt and seduce us into finding goodness and hope through means and venues proffered by the gods and lords of this world.

At stake in this collision is whether or not we will find an authentic, life giving hope that will genuinely sustain and lead us through peril into new life—or will we settle on a false hope that leaves us with immediate good feelings, but ultimately leads us further into death's grip? In short, it is the crisis of placing my trust and confidence in God's bare goodness and

Nourished into New Imagination

future when all the evidence available to my senses gives me no physical or tangible reason to do so. It is the crisis of faith—if we risk calling a thing what it is—that I suspect most of us find ourselves in these days. Faith, as Luther said, must always "have something to believe in—something to which it may cling and upon which it may stand."[1] Just like in borderland reality, the visible and tangible signs offered by the present environment do not offer us much on which faith can cling or stand.

Might it be, however, that this crisis of faith is not because the visible and tangible signs for which we are searching are absent. Rather it is because we are searching for those signs through our own human eyes and ears that have been shaped by our culture's narcissistic and preoccupation with self. In short it is a preoccupation that looks for God in signs that she will return things to what they were—the way I want them to be—rather than in signs that suggest God's power may be about change that is leading us into a future we cannot yet see. We look for signs and validations that will give us comfort and assurance on our terms. We want God to deliver us from our perils on our terms and according to our expectations. When God does not deliver as we expect, we either give in to despair, or find something on which our faith can stand and to which it can cling, even if it is a false security. We have difficulty imagining a God who is beyond our expectations of who God is and what God is supposed to do, especially in the face of peril and threat.

We return to Brueggemann's exposition of Psalm 77, referenced earlier in chapter four. This is the Psalm in which the speaker gives voice to his deep complaint, "And I say, that it is my grief that the power of the Most High has changed."[2] Brueggemann observes that we do not know the life circumstances that have precipitated this complaint; however, we can assume that the speaker's expectation that God in God's power was to have returned things to the way they were have not been fulfilled. God has not intervened or acted as he expected, precipitating his complaint and grief that God's power has changed, or in other words, God's power has not done what it was supposed to do. The speaker's words voiced in this Psalm reflect the same crisis of faith of which we are speaking, the crisis of having faith and hope in God's future when everything in the present moment gives our self-centered senses nothing on which faith can stand or to which it can cling.

---

1. *TLC*, 393.
2. Ps 77:10, NRSV.

Part II: Becoming What We Are Yet to Be

Having said that, Brueggemann's reading of Psalm 77 suggests that the problem is not about an absence of visible or tangible signs. It is the preoccupation with self that looks for God through the eyes of what it wants and expect of God, not through the eyes of a faith that knows God is free to be and act on God's terms. As we have noted, how God chooses to be and act will always be hidden from the purviews and perspectives of our human senses, as the cross testifies. From Brueggemann's viewpoint, the key to understanding this Psalm is the speaker's shift in perspective and attitude, a shift seen between vv. 1–10 and vs. 11. It is a move Brueggemann characterizes as a shift from the speaker's preoccupation with self to a focus on God; it is seen in the the fact that the first ten verses of this Psalm are all about "I," while in the verses that follow the focus is on the "Thou" of God, the "otherness of God," the God whose power has now changed.[3] The shift is evidenced in the speaker's newfound willingness to place his future in the hands of this God who has evidenced herself in the words and deeds of past actions not in whether or not she meets his expectations in the present moment. Brueggemann notes, "The move from vv. 1–10 to vs. 11 is like the move envisioned by Jesus: For whoever would save his life will lose it, but whoever loses his life for the sake of the gospel's will save it (Mark 8:35)."[4]

The shift in the speakers's attitude and posture towards God is marked by a reflection on God's works and deeds of the past in vv 11–12, a contemplation that leads him to conclude that "Your way, O God, is holy. What god is so great as our God?"[5] It is a past that he has forgotten, neglected and otherwise ignored because of his self-preoccupation for things to return to the way they were. As Brueggemann insightfully observes, it is in this reflection on God's works and deeds of the past that

> the speaker comes to the fresh awareness that it is precisely God's freedom to change and come and go that is the hope of Israel and the hope of deliverance of folks like the speaker in this present or any present.[6]

Whatever else happens in the speaker's contemplative reflection on God's past actions, the most important turn is in the speaker's imagination. No this is not an imagination of fantasy or wish fulfillment. If it were,

---

3. Brueggemann, *Virus as a Summons to Faith*, 53.
4. Brueggemann, *Virus as a Summons to Faith*, 53.
5. Ps 77:14, NRSV.
6. Brueggemann, *Virus as a Summons to Faith*, 53.

Nourished into New Imagination

it would simply be another manifestation of the speaker's preoccupation with self. Instead, it is a reimagining of God and a reimagining of who he is in relationship to God. As Brueggemann says of what the speaker has discovered, "God's way is "wholly other," not to be reduced, not to be accommodated or conformed to my needs or my expectations."[7] Instead, this reimagining opens the door to a new faith. It is still a faith in the very same God and it is a faith that God will deliver him, but that deliverance will be on God's terms and in God's way; it is not a deliverance that will be conformed to the speaker's expectations. It is a deliverance that may well be beyond the speaker's comprehension and one that surprises him, perhaps even exasperates him, but it will be a deliverance none the less.

Brueggemann's comments about the end of this Psalm is indispensable to this discussion on where we find faith and hope when there are no tangible signs available to offer us assurance. As he observes, there is no resolution whatsoever to the predicaments or circumstances giving rise to the Psalmist's complaint. What changes is a "recontextualizing" of the complaint itself. The "narrow religious window," which the psalmist presents when all he is preoccupied with is "I" is shattered. It is shattered by remembering, by awareness of God's incomparability, by reference to Israel's concrete history, but most of all it is shattered by the utterance, *Thou*."[8] Brueggemann's conclusion to his exposition speaks directly to the faith crisis we have identified in our present moment.

> The rhetorical cannot be accidental. The contrast is total, decisive, and intentional. And the turn is in vs. 10. Everything is up for grabs in vs. 10 waiting for fresh resolution. It is the pastoral moment that could go either way. It is the evangelical moment in which the news may break. It is the moment of deciding to live in the world where the Most High changes, or to retreat back into the world where the "least high" keeps us at the center of things. It is the pastoral task to be present to that moment of terror, a moment that requires enormous imagination.[9]

Applying Brueggemann's insight to our present moment where death is closer than we thought and where we are besieged by perils and threats on many fronts, the pastoral moment is not to retreat into our survival modes of existence that keep us preoccupied with self and self-survival.

---

7. Brueggemann, *Virus as a Summons to Faith*, 54.
8. Brueggemann, *Virus as a Summons to Faith*, 55.
9. Brueggemann, *Virus as a Summons to Faith*, 55.

Like the speaker in Psalm 77, it is the moment to stay present in these perils and threats, yet to recall and ponder God's works, deeds, and saving acts of the past, not the least of which is the cross of Jesus the Christ. Like the speaker, it is the moment to allow this reflection to lead us into yielding our self-centered "I" to the "Thou" and wholly otherness, of God. As Brueggemann so rightly observes, it is this new faith that leads us into a new obedience, one that is not based on the quid-pro-quo of gaining God's favor or manipulating God to conform to our needs and expectations, but on the clear awareness and hope that God is God on God's terms. In the context of our discussion, it is the faith that opens up our imagination to leave survival and step into baptismal vocation.

Word and Sacrament—Nourishment for New Imaginations

Reflecting on the speaker's transition from the self-centered preoccupation with "I" to a discovery of God's "Thou," Brueggemann was quite clear: it was difficult and it did not come easy. Nor is it easy for us.

> We do not know how any faith-speaker makes the leap from from the preoccupation with self to an imaginative acknowledgement of the primacy of the other. But that is what happens in the psalm and in all serious biblical faith. It involves leaving the safety of "the torah so righteous" for "the God so near" who is yet so free (Deut 4:7–8). The dramatic move concerns the abandonment of self as the primal agenda for the Thou who is out beyond us in freedom. And we make no mistake to observe that that transfer of the agenda, that ceding of concern for self to the other is the crucial move of biblical faith . . . And we observe what an urgent, difficult task Christian nurture and preaching now is. For the narcissism of our culture is precisely aimed at *not* ceding self, not relinquishing. This Psalm (Psalm 77) models the very move of faith that our cultural ideology wants to prevent. The whole consumer perspective concerns retention of self and satiation of self.[10]

Brueggemann's words concerning the urgency of the difficult task of Christian nurture in our present moment is paramount to our discussion. Leaving survival modes of existence and relinquishing the primacy of self to the God who is so totally other and beyond us, yet so very near, is the

---

10. Brueggemann, *Virus as a Summons to Faith,* 51.

very move to which our biblical faith is calling us. But it does not come without nourishment.

Luther understood this need for nourishment. In his explanation to the third commandment, he admonishes the laity to attend to the regular and disciplined hearing of the Word, not as a matter of quid-pro-quo as though it will earn points, but as a matter of necessity for living in a world where the powers of death and evil will always chip away at one's faith and hope, where the cultural powers of narcissism will always beckon us back to the primacy and preoccupation with self. Hear his words.

> Even though you know the word perfectly and have already mastered everything, you are daily under the dominion of the devil who does not rest day or night in seeking to take you unaware and to kindle in your heart unbelief and wicked thoughts . . . Therefore you must constantly keep God's word in your heart, on your lips, and in your ears. For where the heart stands idle and the word is not heard, the devil breaks in and does its damage before we realize it. On the other hand, when we seriously ponder the word, hear it and put it to use, such is its power that it never departs without fruit. It always awakens new understanding, pleasure, and devotion, and it constantly creates clear hearts and minds. For this word is not idle or dead, but effective and living.[11]

Yes, his admonition is cast in the language of medieval piety and a world view of the devil as one who is constantly after our soul. But his meaning is the same: "the devil" in our culture is our primacy and preoccupation with the self. Without constant attention and meditation to God's word, our whole being is vulnerable to the damage inflicted when we do not cede that primacy or preoccupation to the Thou and otherness of God.

Referring to the sacrament of Holy Communion and its link with baptism, Luther said:

> Therefore (the sacrament of Holy Communion) is appropriately called food for the soul, for it nourishes and strengthens the new creature. For in the first instance, we are born anew through baptism. However, our human flesh and blood . . . have not lost their old skin. There are so many hindrances and attacks of the devil and the world that we often grow weary and faint and at times we even stumble. Therefore, the Lord's Supper is given as a daily food and sustenance so that faith may be refreshed and strengthened and that it may not succumb in the struggle but become stronger and

11. *TLC*, 314.

stronger. For the new life should be one that develops and makes progress. But it has to suffer a great deal of opposition. The devil is a furious enemy; when it sees that we resist and attack the old creature and when the devil cannot rout us by force, it sneaks and skulks about every turn, trying all kinds of tricks, and does not stop until it has finally worn us out so that we either renounce our faith or lose heart and become indifferent or impatient. For times like these, when our heart feels too sorely pressed, this comfort of the Lord's Supper is given to bring us new strength and refreshment.[12]

Once again, Luther's admonition is cast in the struggle between the "new and old creatures," and "the devil" who is the vicious enemy working to prevent the emergence of a new life. In the language of our discussion, what is this but the struggle to relinquish the primacy and preoccupation of the self to the Thou and totally otherness of God? Referring back to Psalm 77, what is the new creature but the human being who lives in the new awareness and new obedience that comes from yielding to the God who is totally other and beyond, yet so near? And at the heart of this struggle is evil's—the devil's—pernicious attempts to prevent any such submission or relinquishing of the self to the Thou of God. For Luther, it is precisely this struggle that requires the nourishment of Word and Sacrament, for without this nourishment, we cannot prevail.

Whether the Word comes to us in the form of a spoken word from the pulpit or the visible and tangible word given to us in the form of baptism or Holy Communion, it always a word through which the living past and future of our faith break into our present moments of sufferings, travails, and death! For Luther, when either the spoken word or the visible word of the sacraments are heard or received, Jesus the Christ is present. The past deeds and works of God in Jesus' death and resurrection become real and present in the moment. Just as important, the story embodied and held in these sacraments becomes our story. In Word and Sacrament, where God's creating and life giving Word comes in the form of a spoken word or is held within the ordinary elements of water, bread, and wine, we are visibly and tangibly reminded that becoming one with Christ is not in the past tense. Nor is it a future tense reality deferred to life in heaven. It is present tense: *we are one with Christ now and in this moment*, as incomplete as that union might yet be. His death is our death and his rising is ours!

---

12. *TLC*, 407.

Having said that, a word of caution is in order. For all too often in our culture, the image of being one with Jesus is experienced through the filters of a privatized faith. In this privatization, the image of being in union with Christ assures us of personal forgiveness and the comfort of being held in Jesus' arms. To be clear, there is nothing wrong with these images. What is wrong is that they do not go far enough. If personal assurance and comfort is all we get out of being united with Christ in his death and resurrection, then we have missed the move of faith to which Word and Sacrament are calling us and for which they are nourishing us. It is the move to which Brueggemann referred, the dramatic move that concerns the abandonment of self as our primal agenda for the Thou who is out beyond us in freedom.[13]

While the strength and refreshment of Word and Sacrament is for one's inner and personal spirit to be sure, it is not a refreshment and comfort solely intended for private use. Notice Luther's words. It is a nourishment intended to keep us from being worn out, from losing heart, and from becoming indifferent and impatient. It is a nourishment intended to keep us from giving up and falling away from the pilgrimage of being a culture of life in a world of death. Luther knew that if the heart and spirit of a person are not nourished

> . . . harm has to follow and it cannot but happen that (a person's) faith daily becomes increasingly weak and cold; as a result, then, it must furthermore follow that he becomes lazy and cold in his love for neighbor, sluggish and averse to doing good works, unfit and unwilling to resist evil.[14]

In short, without this nourishment, the self retreats into its survival mode of self-preoccupation and self-survival and fails to live into baptismal vocation.

Strength of faith is not just about perseverance through personal hardship. Strength of faith is about persevering through all of the obstacles that hinder our baptismal pilgrimage into vocation. Faith is what emboldens and empowers the heart to carry the burdens and sufferings of others. A cold heart has no capacity to bear another's burdens, to care one way or another whether neighbor is dehumanized or power dominated, or whether the earth's resources are exploited and abused for the sake of self-indulging appetites. A cold heart is capable only of turning inward to give itself self

---

13. Brueggemann, *Virus as a Summons to Faith*, 55.
14. *TLC*, 407.

absorbed satisfaction. When faith is a faith that follows the Thou and otherness of God who in her freedom is leading us into her future, it is a faith that opens our eyes and hearts to realities to the God who is beyond and out in front of us.

Faith and hope in the new creation that has been inaugurated in Jesus the Christ does not allow us to see the world and our neighbor through the old lens of self-absorbed narcissism. As Brueggemann reminded us, it is what empowers us to see possibilities and life alternatives beyond what our limited human senses perceive. Much, then, is at stake when faith grows weak, lazy and cold, hence much is also at stake if the life-giving Word, spoken or held in the ordinary water, bread, and wine of baptism and Holy Communion, is ignored. These are God's gifts, instituted and given by God herself as the means to instill, nourish, and sustain our faith, trust, and hope in the new creation as we stand situated amid the powers of evil and death. They dare not and cannot be ignored if we are to leave survival for the vocation of being a culture of life in the midst of those powers.

Conclusion—Back to Where We Started

Luther's instruction on the sacraments is the last of the four chief parts of both the Large and Small Catechism. In both catechisms, they bring his instruction to a close. However, if we rethink and change how we use his instruction so that it is no longer a one-and-done instruction required for admission into the Lutheran communion but rather an instruction and guide on the life and pilgrimage of leaving survival for vocation, then his instruction on the sacraments, along with what he says about the spoken word, are not a conclusion. Instead, they are the sustaining nourishment that propel us into God's future and new creation. They propel us into the vocational life to which the gospel calls us. They do not allow us to escape into a cocooned world where we can hide from what is happening around us or escape our vocational responsibility to defend our neighbor from harm. In this regard, they take us right back to where this whole discussion started. They propel us back into a world where death is closer than we thought. Yet they propel us into that world with a renewed sense of identity, purpose, and hope, all of which empower us to engage the world and its sufferings as transforming agents rather than retreat from it. Whether to trust the identity that has been given so as to engage what we are up against—or not to trust and retreat—will always be the existential vocational question with which we daily come up against.

A brief story will illustrate. As this story goes, there was once a lifesaving mission on a seacoast that was notorious for its dangerous storms, storms that threatened the life of many a sailor and ship. The lifesaving mission had become famous for its work of venturing into dangerous and risky seas to save lives from peril and harm. The mission itself began in a crude hut with few members, yet even with its limited facilities and resources, it was able to fulfill the purpose for which it had been organized—to protect sailors whose lives were threatened from harm, danger, and death. As its fame and reputation grew, many came to join in its work and mission, so that after a while, new facilities were needed to house its growing membership. And so new facilities were built, only this time, the facilities included comfortable accommodations where members could relax when they were not out on the dangerous seas saving lives. In time, their concern for maintaining the building and its comforts took priority over saving lives. The facilities became a kind of club. However, those who remained faithful to the mission and vocation of risking their own lives to save the lives of others eventually left and built themselves a new facility to house their work. But once again, as new people came to join in their mission, new facilities were needed and built, and once again comfort took priority over the work of saving lives. This pattern continued for some time so that now when travelers drive along this coast, they will see many clubs and wonderful facilities, yet many lives are now lost.[15]

This is our present danger as a church situated in a self-absorbed narcissistic culture. It is the danger of turning our hearts inward to serve the self-preoccupations of our "I" rather than give ourselves over to the "Thou" of God who is out in front of us and in her freedom calling us to take the risks of living into her future. It is the danger of serving our "I", at the expense of ignoring the cries of those who are in the throes and grasp of evil and death's power. It is the danger of prioritizing our comfort over the cries of those who suffer from racism's dehumanizing hate, from the earth's groans and gasps for life, from the cries of those suffering from exploitation and domination in whatever form those come. Yet if we listen closely, the gospel's radical and relevant call in our present moment is that we are being sent out "like lambs into the midst of wolves."[16] It will always be tempting to

15. Clinebell, *Basic Types of Pastoral Counseling*, 1.
16. Luke 10:1–11, NRSV.

Part II: Becoming What We Are Yet to Be

stay inside where the wolves, or the stormy seas, will not harm us. But that is exactly why we pray,

> Holy, Creating, and Life Sustaining God, In the midst of ravenous wolves, deathly seas, and anything else that causes us fear and dread, empower us to *keep your name holy* by leaving behind our preoccupations with "I," and taking the risks to follow your "Thou." In all that we do, equip us to be faithful to the new creation and vocation into which you are daily calling us, even when it means taking risks. Help us to keep your name holy by not retreating from the cross when we are asked to bear it.
>
> *Let your your culture of life in the midst of death—your kingdom—come*; let us be your kingdom and not just people who talk about it. *Let your will be done* and come to fruition in all of our interactions with our neighbors, the world, and creation itself. Let us not stay content with good intentions, thinking that we have done enough. Equip us to turn those intentions into good works of justice, peace, and mercy.
>
> Holy God, *give us what we need for the day*, not just the bread we eat, but the very environment we need for there to be a just, fair, and equitable world. Where there is hatred, equip us with what we need to be transforming agents of mercy; where there is injustice, equip us with what we need to advocate for justice and fairness. Where there is abuse of the earth, equip us with what we need to be advocates for its health and welfare, for without the earth, we can have no life at all.
>
> Holy one, every day we step into a world that breathes the air of hateful judgmentalism, retribution and retaliation, a world that breathes the air of getting even, a world that breathes the air of grudges, long held angers and resentments. Equip *us with the air of forgiveness that we might offer grace instead of hateful judgment, reconciliation instead of retribution, that we might be free from the grudges and resentment that burden and oppress our lives and the lives of our neighbors.*
>
> Holy God, *lead us not into the temptation of seeking comfort over your vocational call that asks us to take risks and venture into unknown places.* Lead us not into the temptation of easy and quick fixes that will bring us immediate relief but in the end do nothing but leave us empty. And especially keep us from the temptation of giving up hope in your faithfulness to your promises.

And now, especially in this time where death is so imminently close, *keep us from harm and danger.* And even if we should be overtaken by the powers of evil and death, hold our spirit and give us the never ending vision that we are always held in your eternal grasp. For indeed we are held in your grasp, because yours is the power and the glory forever. Amen! Amen! And Amen!

As a final blessing for all of us as we step into our pilgrimage of leaving survival for vocation and becoming what we are yet to be—a culture of life in the face of death—I once again defer to the powerful words of Jürgen Moltmann:

> In the eternal yes of the living God, we affirm our fragile and vulnerable humanity in spite of death; in the eternal love of God, we love life and resist its devastations; in the ungraspable nearness of God, we trust in what is saving, even if the dangers are growing.[17]

And may it be so for all of us!

---

17. Moltmann, *Spirit of Hope*, 14.

Bibliography

Alanís, Javier. "Living in Third Spaces." http://jayalanis.com/wp-content/uploads/2018/12/Living-in-Third-Spaces%0B-Ohio-Leadership-Conference-2019.pdf.

Boorstein, Michelle. "Researchers Warn That Christian Nationalists Are Becoming More Radical and Are Targeting Voting." *The Washington Post*, March 18, 2022. https://www.washingtonpost.com/religion/2022/03/18/white-christian-nationalism-raskin-tlaib-democracy-freethought-secular/.

Brooks, David. "When a Heart Is Empty." *The New York Times*, September 10, 2020. https://www.nytimes.com/2020/09/10/opinion/trump-coronavirus-military-comments.html. September 10, 2020.

Brueggemann, Walter. *Finally Comes the Poet: Daring Speech for Proclamation.* Minneapolis: Fortress, 1989.

———. *Gift and Task: A Year of Daily Readings and Reflections.* Louisville: Westminster John Knox, 2017.

———. *Praying the Psalms: Engaging Scripture and the Life of the Spirit.* 2nd ed. Eugene, OR: Cascade, 2007.

———. *Virus as a Summons to Faith.* Eugene, OR: Cascade, 2020.

Carter, Warren. *Matthew and the Margins: A Sociopolitical and Religious Reading.* The Bible and Liberation Series. Maryknoll: Orbis, 2000.

Clinebell, Howard. *Basic Types of Pastoral Counseling.* San Francisco: Harper & Row, 1981.

Cone, James H. *The Cross and the Lynching Tree.* Maryknoll: Orbis, 2011.

Day, Dorothy. "83 Notable Quotes." https://quotes.thefamouspeople.com/dorothy-day-1255.php

Dole, Robert. "Presidential Election Concession Speech." https://www.presidency.ucsb.edu/documents/presidential-election-concession-speech.

Ellul, Jacques. *Living Faith,* Translated by Peter Heinegg. San Francisco: Harper & Row, 1983.

Bibliography

Friedman, Edwin. *A Failure of Nerve: Leadership in an Age of Quick Fix*. Edited by Margaret M. Treadwell and Edward W. Beal. New York: Seabury, 2007.

The Guardian. "Mother of a California Shooting Victim." YouTube video, 0:0:37. November 9, 2018. http:youtube.com/watch?v=f8Jt7E8XmRQ.

Gerson, Michael. "The GOP Is Now Just the Party of White Grievance." *The Washington Post*, March 1, 2021. https://www.washingtonpost.com/opinions/the-gop-is-now-just-the-party-of-white-grievance/2021/03/01/67679480-7ab9-11eb-85cd-9b7fa90c8873_story.html.

Hall, Douglas John. *Imaging God: Dominion as Stewardship*. Eugene, OR: Wipf & Stock, 2004. Previously published as *Imaging God: Dominion as Stewardship*. Grand Rapids: Eerdmans, 1986.

———. *Lighten Our Darkness: Towards and Indigenous Theology of the Cross*. Philadelphia: Westminster, 1976.

Kretzschmar, Louise. "The Privatization of the Christian Faith." *Baptist Quarterly* 38 (1999) 128–33.

Lasch, Christopher. *The Culture of Narcissism*. New York: Norton, 1978.

Moltmann, Jurgen. *The Spirit of Hope: Theology for a World in Peril*. Louisville: Westminster John Knox, 2019.

Moore, Lemar. "Survival Mode Is Killing You." https://mastermindconnect.com/blog/survival-mode-is-killing-you.

Nessan, Craig. *Free in Deed: The Heart of Lutheran Ethics*. Minneapolis: Fortress, 2022.

Ogbazor. "Martin Luther King, Jr." https://blogs.shu.edu/diplomacyresearch/2013/12/31/martin-luther-king-jr/.

Palmer, Parker. *The Courage to Teach: Exploring the Inner Landscape of a Teacher's Life*. San Francisco: Josey-Bass, 1998.

Sitler, Joseph. *Gravity and Grace: Reflections and Provocations*. Edited by Linda-Marie Delloff. Minneapolis: Augsburg, 1986. Quoted in Mary M. Solberg. *Compelling Knowledge: A Feminist Proposal for an Epistemology of the Cross*. Albany: State University of New York Press, 1997.

Solberg, Mary M. *Compelling Knowledge: A Feminist Proposal for an Epistemology of the Cross*. Albany: State University of New York Press, 1997.

Tappert, Theodore, ed. *The Book of Concord*. Philadelphia: Fortress, 1959.

Washington State University. "Consumption by the United States." https://public.wsu.edu/~mreed/380American%20Consumption.html.

Wheeler, Kenneth. "Little By Little Is No Longer Enough." *Living Lutheran* 6 (2021) 38–39. https://pubs.royle.com/publication/?m=62112&i=720713&p=38&ver=html5.

"White Collar Crime." https://www.fbi.gov/investigate/white-collar-crime.

Wigmore, Ivy. "Internet Shaming." https://www.techtarget.com/whatis/definition/internet-shaming.

Zubatov, Alexander. "We Are Living in the Ruins of Our Civilization." https://amgreatness.com/2021/02/24/we-are-living-in-the-ruins-of-our-civilization/.

Made in the USA
Coppell, TX
14 February 2023